THE ORIGINS OF
THE SECOND WORLD WAR:

A. J. P. Taylor and His Critics

MAJOR ISSUES IN HISTORY

Editor

C. WARREN HOLLISTER

University of California, Santa Barbara

William F. Church: *The Impact of Absolutism in France: National Experience under Richelieu, Mazarin, and Louis XIV*

Robert O. Collins: *The Partition of Africa: Illusion or Necessity*

J. B. Conacher: *The Emergence of Parliamentary Democracy in Britain in the Nineteenth Century*

Gerald D. Feldman: *German Imperialism, 1914–1918: The Development of A Historical Debate*

Frank J. Frost: *Democracy and the Athenians*

Paul Hauben: *The Spanish Inquisition*

Bennett D. Hill: *Church and State in the Middle Ages*

Boyd H. Hill: *The Rise of the First Reich: Germany in the Tenth Century*

C. Warren Hollister: *The Impact of the Norman Conquest*

C. Warren Hollister: *The Twelfth-Century Renaissance*

James C. Holt: *Magna Carta and the Idea of Liberty*

Thomas M. Jones: *The Becket Controversy*

Tom B. Jones: *The Sumerian Problem*

Jeffrey Kaplow: *France on the Eve of Revolution*

Archibald Lewis: *Islamic World and the West*

Wm. Roger Louis: *The Origins of the Second World War: A. J. P. Taylor and His Critics*

Leonard Marsak: *The Enlightenment*

Anthony Molho: *Social and Economic Foundations of the Italian Renaissance*

E. W. Monter: *European Witchcraft*

Donald Queller: *The Latin Conquest of Constantinople*

Joachim Remak: *The First World War: Causes, Conduct, Consequences*

Jeffry Russell: *Religious Dissent in the Middle Ages*

Max Salvadori: *European Liberalism*

W. M. Simon: *French Liberalism, 1789–1848*

Arthur J. Slavin: *Humanism, Reform, and Reformation*

W. Warren Wagar: *The Idea of Progress Since the Renaissance*

Bertie Wilkinson: *The Creation of Medieval Parliaments*

L. Pearce Williams: *Relativity Theory: Its Origins and Impact on Modern Thought*

Roger L. Williams: *The Commune of Paris, 1871*

Martin Wolfe: *The Economic Causes of Imperialism*

THE ORIGINS OF
THE SECOND
WORLD WAR:
A. J. P. Taylor and His Critics

EDITED BY

Wm. Roger Louis

University of Texas

John Wiley & Sons, Inc.

New York • London • Sydney • Toronto

Library of Congress Cataloging in Publication Data:

Louis, Wm. Roger.
The Origins of the Second World War.

(Major issues in history)
1. Taylor, Alan John Percivale, 1906-   The Origins of the Second World War.   I. Title.

D741.L65 1972   940.53′11′0924   72-2455
ISBN 0-471-54469-8
ISBN 0-471-54473-6 (pbk.)

Printed in the United States of America

10 9 8 7 6 5 4 3 2 1

To my friend C. Hartley Grattan, one of the leading "revisionists" of the *First* World War

SERIES PREFACE

The reading program in a history survey course traditionally has consisted of a large two-volume textbook and, perhaps, a book of readings. This simple reading program requires few decisions and little imagination on the instructor's part, and tends to encourage in the student the virtue of careful memorization. Such programs are by no means things of the past, but they certainly do not represent the wave of the future.

The reading program in survey courses at many colleges and universities today is far more complex. At the risk of oversimplification, and allowing for many exceptions and overlaps, it can be divided into four categories: (1) textbook, (2) original source readings, (3) specialized historical essays and interpretive studies, and (4) historical problems.

After obtaining an overview of the course subject matter (textbook), sampling the original sources, and being exposed to selective examples of excellent modern historical writing (historical essays), the student can turn to the crucial task of weighing various possible interpretations of major historical issues. It is at this point that memory gives way to creative critical thought. The "problems approach," in other words, is the intellectual climax of a thoughtfully conceived reading program and is, indeed, the most characteristic of all approaches to historical pedagogy among the newer generation of college and university teachers.

The historical problems books currently available are many and varied. Why add to this information explosion? Because the Wiley Major Issues Series constitutes an endeavor to produce something new that will respond to pedagogical needs thus far unmet. First, it is a series of individual volumes—one per problem. Many good teachers would much prefer to select their own historical issues rather than be tied to an inflexible sequence of issues imposed by a publisher and bound together between two covers. Second, the Wiley Major Issues Series is based on the idea of approaching the significant problems of history through a deft interweaving of primary sources and secondary analysis, fused together by the skill of a scholar-editor. It is felt that the essence of a historical issue cannot be satisfactorily probed either by placing a body of undigested source materials into the hands of inexperienced students or by limiting these students to the controversial literature of modern scholars who debate the meaning of sources the student never sees. This series approaches historical problems by exposing students to both the finest historical thinking on the issue and some of the evidence on which this thinking is based. This synthetic approach should prove far more fruitful than either the raw-source approach or the exclusively second-hand approach, for it combines the advantages— and avoids the serious disadvantage—of both.

Finally, the editors of the individual volumes in the Major Issues Series have been chosen from among the ablest scholars in their fields. Rather than faceless referees, they are historians who know their issues from the inside and, in most instances, have themselves contributed significantly to the relevant scholarly literature. It has been the editorial policy of this series to permit the editor-scholars of the individual volumes the widest possible latitude both in formulating their topics and in organizing their materials. Their scholarly competence has been unquestioningly respected; they have been encouraged to approach the problems as they see fit. The titles and themes of the series volumes have been suggested in nearly every case by the scholar-editors themselves. The criteria have been (1) that the issue be of relevance to undergraduate lecture courses in history, and (2) that it be an issue which the scholar-editor knows thoroughly and in which he has done creative work. And, in general, the second criterion has been given precedence over the first. In short, the question "What are the significant historical issues today?" has been answered not by general editors or sales departments but by the scholar-teachers who are responsible for these volumes.

University of California,   *C. Warren Hollister*
Santa Barbara

CONTENTS

From Valhalla, Hitler congratulates Mr. Taylor on his book.
Magdalen College of Oxford University is in the background.
© Copyright 1962 by American Heritage Publishing Co., Inc.
Reprinted by permission from *Horizon Magazine*, March 1962.
Illustration by Tom Allen.

A. J. P. Taylor: A Biographical Sketch

Alan John Percivale Taylor was born eight years before the outbreak of the First World War, about which he has published a spectacular illustrated history. Educated at a Quaker school and Oriel College, Oxford, he later studied diplomatic history at the University of Vienna and from 1930 to 1938 lectured at the University of Manchester. From 1938 to 1963 he was a tutorial Fellow of Magdalen College, Oxford, during which time he acquired a reputation as a prolific writer, intellectual gad-fly, stimulating teacher, and foremost authority of diplomatic history. A Fellow of the British Academy, he is presently a Research Fellow of Magdalen College and Honorary Director of the Beaverbrook Library in London. His books include a study of Italian diplomatic history, a work on the Habsburg monarchy, a biography of Bismarck, and the standard account of European diplomatic history, *The Struggle for Mastery in Europe, 1848–1918*. In 1945 he published an intensely anti-German book, *The Course of German History*. Often described as a professional "thrower of banana skins," Mr. Taylor frequently upsets his colleagues by taking unorthodox positions and challenging accepted historical interpretations. He prides himself on being a journalist as well as an historian; he lectures on television and contributes to the *Sunday Express* a regular column that some of his colleagues consider to be outrageous because of its outspoken pro-Soviet and anti-Common Market opinions. He also supports the cause of unilateral disarmament, but, alas, he has not written about it.

These maverick activities reputedly contributed to his failure to be appointed Regius Professor at Oxford, a post that went to Hugh Trevor-Roper, despite strong sentiment in favor of Mr. Taylor. Most people assume that Professor Trevor-Roper is Mr. Taylor's archrival. According to Mr. Taylor, this is not true. In his own words: "Trevor-Roper is not my rival. He happened to get the Regius Chair, but in my opinion he is not a twentieth-century historian and therefore no rival. I once told a newspaper: 'He knows as much about the twentieth century as I do about the seventeenth, which is not nothing.' Unfortunately it appeared as 'nothing.' "

Mr. Taylor's critics claim that his impish wit mars his historical writing, which is characterized by brisk clearness and paradox. His present historical philosophy (as of March 23, 1972) is that "the study of history enables us to understand the past better, no more and no less." In the past, however, he has offended many historians by his often stated assertion that the sole purpose of history is to amuse.

In any case, when he published *The Origins of the Second World War* in 1961, many critics definitely were not amused. Far from accepting the conventional interpretations of the origins of the war, Mr. Taylor put forward these, among other, arguments: Hitler had no precise preconceived plans for war in 1939; the immediate outbreak of the war was the fault of British and French diplomats as well as Hitler himself; Hitler was merely a typical German, though perhaps more inflated with grandiose ideas; the war of 1939–1945 can only be objectively assessed with an attitude of historical curiosity; and the British policy of appeasement was enlightened and well-intended, if ineffective. Mr. Taylor himself, it should be noted, was not an appeaser. "Before World War II," he has written, "I was both an active anti-Nazi and an active antiappeaser, a great deal more active in fact than most of my critics." Many of his harshest critics are Americans. In this regard I asked him to provide us with a provocative thought to end this biographical sketch. He failed not: "What right have American historians especially to criticize me when their own country would never have entered the war if Hitler had not casually declared war on it?"

Introduction

This book contains the major critical reviews of A. J. P. Taylor's *The Origins of the Second World War*. The purpose of reproducing them as a symposium is to have a convenient guide to the most substantial—and bitter—controversy about the origins of World War II, and, by examining the arguments in the critiques, to clarify the causes of the war itself.

As Harry Elmer Barnes has commented, nothing comparable by an English author has been written since the "revisionist" E. D. Morel attacked Sir Edward Grey's diplomacy. It is, as he has observed, a "historical shocker." The book stands alone as the only major "revisionist" interpretation of the European (as distinct from Asian or American) causes of World War II. Critics have praised it as brilliant and objective, while others have censured it as mischievous and irresponsible. Mr. Taylor, on the one hand, has been compared with Gibbon and Macaulay, and on the other, denounced as an unscrupulous apologist for Hitler and appeasement. Some critics have pointed out that the book is an effort to reconstruct the events leading to war as they might appear "to some future historian, working from the records." Others have questioned whether such a profound issue can be adequately treated within the framework of diplomatic history. To give but one example of the discrepancy in opinion about the value of Mr. Taylor's work, the reviewer in *The Times Literary Supplement* praised it for its "methodical and impeccable logic," while the reviewer in the *American Historical Review* attacked the book for its internal contradictions and "manipulation of the evidence." In these contradictory evaluations can be found various definitions of "revisionist" history. Most of Mr. Taylor's critics use the word in a pejorative sense—a "rewrite" at variance with historical truth. Mr. Taylor appears to use "revision" in a positive sense implying that historical events should be continually reassessed; specifically, "revision" in the *Origins* means, in his own words, "suggesting that Hitler used different methods from those usually attributed to him."

The indictment against Mr. Taylor can be summarized by stating that he "whitewashed" Hitler and defended the "appeasement" policy of Great Britain. The theme of "apologia for Hitler" runs through many of the critiques. In the *Origins* Hitler is depicted in some ways as a serious and rational statesman; by doing so Mr. Taylor challenges one of the basic tenets of many historians who have assumed Hitler's fundamental irrationality. To say that Hitler was a madman who masterminded the war, or was "just insane," according to Mr. Taylor, is too easy an answer. One of the major themes of the book can be seen as a search for the rational basis of Hitler's policy as it developed against the background of German history.

The second major charge, that Mr. Taylor misunderstands the nature and intention of British policy, can perhaps be simply put by mentioning the ire of the critics at the statement that the Munich agreement was "a triumph for all that was best and most enlightened in British life." In an additional chapter in the second edition, Mr. Taylor comments that he should have written in parenthesis "goak here" after that sentence—suggesting that his critics failed to see the vein of irony running through the book. Defenders of Mr. Taylor's work are quick to point out that the subtlety of his writing eluded many of the reviewers. His critics reply that light treatment of so serious a subject demonstrates his untrustworthiness as a historian. In any case the controversy has caused more debate about the meaning of "appeasement" than any similar historical exchange since the war.

Whatever the validity of the charges against Mr. Taylor, there can be no doubt that the controversy has raised basic questions that go to the heart of the historical discipline: the use of evidence, the role of the historian in society and as a teacher, and the meaning of "revision" in history. Above all the book raises the issue of chance and determination. Historians have usually held that Hitler carefully planned and perpetrated the war, leaving nothing to chance. Mr. Taylor argues that Hitler, like everyone else, was "too absorbed by events to follow a preconceived plan." In short, the outbreak of the war occurred by chance. Hitler may have had a grand design in the sense of a "lunatic vision"; but he had no intention of becoming involved in war with Britain and France in 1939. In other words, Hitler and the Germans in general may ultimately have caused the war, but they did not want it to start when it did—which is quite different from saying that they did not want war at all. The critics reply to this line of argument by charging that Mr. Taylor has failed to take sufficient account of basic documentary evidence such as *Mein Kampf*.

I shall not attempt to outline the varied aspects of controversy raised by Mr. Taylor's book (they become vividly clear in the critiques), but will merely say a word about the way I have organized the essays. They do not appear in strict chronological order, though they do fall roughly into English and American halves to correspond with the dates of publication (April 1961 in the United Kingdom, January 1962 in the United States). I have interspersed newspapers and magazine reviews with scholarly critiques to indicate how the debate developed in different ways and to provide a convenient means of comparison between the reviews of professional historians and those by professional journalists. In conformity with the editorial policy of this series, I have omitted footnotes; they may be easily traced by reference to the original publications.

The first essay, by Edward B. Segel, gives a balanced account of Mr. Taylor's historical philosophy in relation to the origins of World War II. It also contains biographical information about Mr. Taylor. Citations of similar essays—and to other commentaries on the *Origins*—may be found in the "suggestions for further reading" at the end of the book.

The next selection, a memorandum from Hitler in Valhalla to Taylor in Oxford, I include at the beginning because it is the most furiously emotional response to the *Origins* (though Professor Trevor-Roper's commentary is also quite emotional). Mr. Taylor is erroneously referred to as a "Professor" (as in several other reviews). As can be seen from the frontispiece, he is depicted with an iron cross against the background of Magdalen College, Oxford.

The genesis of the controversy is in the section from *The Times*

Literary Supplement. The anonymous reviewer praised the *Origins* as "devastating, superlatively readable, and deeply disturbing." In any case it was indeed deeply disturbing, for the reviewer (presumably E. H. Carr) drew the wrath of some of England's most distinguished scholars of modern European history. Mr. Taylor characteristically refused to reply to his antagonists and merely thanked them for the free publicity they gave to his book.

The *Origins* received mixed reactions in such periodicals as the *Economist,* the *Listener,* and the *New Statesman,* and the reviewer in *International Affairs* apparently thought Mr. Taylor had attempted a gigantic hoax by inventing "imaginable history." On the other hand, Professor Hugh Trevor-Roper, far from regarding the book as a joke, savaged the book in *Encounter.* Another reviewer, A. L. Rowse of Oxford, referred to Trevor-Roper's review as "the most devastating analysis that I have ever seen." Trevor-Roper concluded that the *Origins* is "utterly erroneous" and, by supporting neo-Nazi mythology, would do "harm, perhaps irreparable harm, to Mr. Taylor's reputation as a serious historian."

In one of the most abstract of the critiques, F. H. Hinsley of Cambridge questions Mr. Taylor's success in identifying the "profound causes" of the war and discusses the distinctions between general policy and precise planning, and cause and occasions. G. F. Hudson of Oxford broaches the same questions and, by drawing on passages from *Mein Kampf* and evidence such as the "Hossbach memorandum," directly challenges Mr. Taylor's thesis that Hitler had no explicit plans for war. He concludes that had history occurred as Mr. Taylor conceives it, "in company probably with Mr. Taylor himself we should long ago have perished in Buchenwald or Dachau."

When the book appeared in the United States in January 1962, it received an even more hostile reception than in England—according to Mr. Taylor, because American professors dislike revising their lecture notes. Professor Gordon Craig of Stanford in the *New York Times* labelled the book "perverse." A. L. Rowse in the *New York Herald Tribune* responded in particular to the statement that the origins of the war was "a story without heroes, and perhaps without villains" by writing that Taylor was "at pains to whittle down Hitler's responsibility at every point."

Time took the same line: "no one (outside Germany) seemed to have thought of scrubbing up Hitler—until now." Serious scholarly reviews appeared by Professors Sontag, Freidel, and Morton. Professor Morton's critique is especially important because it relates Mr. Taylor's "revisionist" theme to major events and interpretations of American history. Harry Elmer Barnes, "one of those raving American revisionists" (Taylor's description), achieved the distinction of being virtually the only American who reviewed the book with unreserved enthusiasm. He concluded: "The Taylor book may well reduce to rags and tatters the blackout blanket in which historical truth has been swaddled for a generation."

I include the essay by Alan Bullock as the last selection because many historians believe that it offers the most searching evaluation of the controversy. He sums up the arguments of the book, those of the principal critics (especially Professor Trevor-Roper's) and presents what many believe to be a balanced interpretation. Mr. Taylor, however, does not agree. I quote from a personal letter, with his permission: "I do not agree that Bullock provides a balanced interpretation of his own. The first edition of his Hitler [biography] has the traditional view that Hitler planned everything. It even accepts the Hossbach protocol. The lecture [the concluding essay in this symposium] accepted every detailed point of mine. Yet at the end Bullock says: "I was right all along. Hitler caused the second world war." As Professor James Joll said to me: "Ingenious to make one reputation by putting forward a view and then to make another by destroying that view."

In a letter to *The Times Literary Supplement,* Professor W. N. Medlicott, a scholar of European diplomatic history, complained that the *Origins* would "confuse undergraduates." I, on the other hand, do not believe that students should be discouraged from reading any work of history, good or bad, accurate or false, serious or mischievous. Whatever the ultimate evaluation of the *Origins,* I think it should be read by every student interested in the events leading to the outbreak of war.[1] I hope that this sym-

---

[1] For student use I recommend the American paperback edition (Fawcett Premier Book M398), which contains a preface for the American reader and a reply by Mr. Taylor to his critics.

posium will be of use in identifying the crucial issues. It should raise questions concerning the responsibility of critics as well as historians (including the important problem of how criticism should and should not be written) and I hope the critiques collectively will be of interest to anyone concerned with the causes of World War II.

* * *

Finally, a short word about A. J. P. Taylor and my own impression of a major aspect of the *Origins* that many of the reviewers have neglected or misunderstood. I have tried to be objective in my remarks above, but I think it best to make my own bias clear. Mr. Taylor, in my opinion, is not only a controversial but also a brilliant historian. I agree with the remark of the reviewer in *The Times Literary Supplement* that "one is left wondering at the perversity which has prevented any university institution in the country from giving a professorial chair to one of England's two or three outstanding historians." I also agree with the *Economist* when, on the publication of Mr. Taylor's *English History* in 1965, it stated that it was a source of embarrassment that he had been slighted in his profession because of the *Origins*. The eclipse of his reputation was brief; it is probably accurate to say that he is now widely regarded as the doyen of English historians.

Perhaps the value of the *Origins* controversy is the series of questions about national psychology that the book raises but does not attempt to answer: If Hitler were a madman, how did he manage to get such a hold over the German people? Why did the Germans follow him as they did? Was Hitler merely a product of his environment? Did he have a "plan"?, and if so did the German people have a free will to follow him? Mr. Taylor's answers to those questions might at first sight appear to be ambiguous, in line with the central ambiguity of the book. The *Origins* can be interpreted in two entirely different ways. In Taylor's own words, "My book *can* be read in two ways. In one way, it may sort of exonerate Hitler by saying the war was a mistake; in another, by letting Hitler off, it may make all Germans responsible for the war."[2] Yet it seems to me perfectly clear that, beneath the ambiguity, the book is profoundly anti-German

---

[2] Quoted in Ved Mehta, *Fly and the Fly-Bottle: Encounters with British Intellectuals* (Boston, ?1963), p. 171.

and that those critics who claim that it is an attempt to white-wash Hitler are entirely wrong. I read the book's main theme as consistent with that of the *Course of German History* (1945), in which Mr. Taylor depicted the Germans as cruel, cunning, warlike, and wicked. In the *Origins* those characteristics are still ascribed to the German nation, though more subtly. For example, in "second thoughts," Mr. Taylor writes: "As supreme ruler of Germany, Hitler bears the greatest responsibility for acts of immeasurable evil: for the destruction of German democracy; for the concentration camps; and, worst of all, for the extermination of peoples during the second World War. He gave orders, which Germans executed, of a wickedness without parallel in civilised history." Hitler, according to Taylor, was a sounding board for the German nation. Throughout the *Origins* Hitler appears merely as a typical German writ large—surely a damning indictment of the German people. But the message has been widely misunderstood. When a taxi driver in Munich asked Mr. Taylor if he was English and Mr. Taylor replied "jawohl," the taxi driver queried whether he knew a certain A. J. P. Taylor. Taylor, taken aback, said that he knew him well, being himself A. J. P. Taylor. The taxi driver stopped in midtraffic, extending his hand to congratulate him for having proved Hitler to be right after all. No one, I am sure, has ever been more chagrined than Alan Taylor!

Since Mr. Taylor and his critics lived through the "Hitler years" (and some through the "First German War" of 1914–1918), it is understandable how the controversy has generated such bitter emotion. Now that there is a generation of students who were not yet born when Hitler met his end, it should be possible for younger historians to take a fresh look at the whole story without the emotional background unavoidable for the generation that experienced World War II. The overriding purpose of this volume is to present both sides of the controversy in relation to Mr. Taylor's own single, challenging interpretation. It will be up to the younger generation of historians to answer the basic question raised by the essays. As posed by Alan Bullock, "Is Mr. A. J. P. Taylor the harbinger of a new generation of revisionist historians who will find it as anachronistic to hold Hitler—or anyone else—responsible for the outbreak of the Second World War as to hold the Kaiser responsible for the outbreak of the First?"

1   *Edward B. Segel*
     A. J. P. Taylor and History

*This article is probably the best introduction to A. J. P.
Taylor's career and the paradoxes of his historical writing.*

A. J. P. Taylor's reputation among his fellow historians, like his
writings, is marked by paradoxes and contradictions. There is
respect for his learning, envy of his brilliance, admiration for his
originality, and irritation, if not downright indignation, at his
alleged vices. In private, his close friends assure you of his very
great qualities as a historian, only to grumble at his absurdities
as a showman. In public, his reviewers, even when they praise his
scholarship, complain of the impossibility of seeing him as a
whole:

"There is something Shavian about A. J. P. Taylor and his
place among academic historians: he is brilliant, erudite, witty,
dogmatic, heretical, irritating, insufferable, and withal inescap-
able. He sometimes insults and always instructs his fellow-histo-
rians. . . ."

Almost ten years have passed since this comment was made, and
Taylor is no less controversial now than before. Indeed, his two

SOURCE. Edward B. Segel, "A. J. P. Taylor and History," October 1964,
The Review of Politics. Reprinted by permission.

latest books, *The Origins of the Second World War* (1961) and the *Illustrated History of the First World War* (1963) have only increased his notoriety among his colleagues. As for this essay, the assumption behind it is that a historian as prolific and important as Taylor deserves a comprehensive and sober analysis, and that perhaps even his eccentricity and insufferableness can be instructive.

Alan John Percivale Taylor has had a long and generally successful career—or set of careers, one might say. He was born in 1906 in Lancashire, the only son of a well-to-do Radical-Liberal cotton manufacturer. After attending a Quaker school (Bootham) in York, Taylor went on to Oriel College, Oxford, where he prided himself in being the only member of the Labour Club in the college. After obtaining a degree in history with First Class Honours, he studied diplomatic history under A. F. Pribram in Vienna, and then moved on to Manchester as a lecturer in modern history. In these years at Manchester (1930–38) he first met Lewis Namier, who remained an important personal influence in Taylor's life and thinking. Since 1938 Taylor has been at Oxford as a Fellow of Magdalen College and (until 1963) a university lecturer—in recent years attracting both a large following of undergraduates and a noisy buzz of gossip. He has never been appointed to a university chair; when the Regius Professorship was most recently filled, H. R. Trevor-Roper, not Taylor, was the appointee, and the commonroom accounts attributed this, ironically, to Namier's influence. Other honors have not been lacking, however; in 1956 Taylor was elected to the British Academy, and he has held several honorary lectureships from both Oxford and Cambridge. His popularity at Oxford was not shaken—and may well have been enhanced—by the controversy he aroused, and his reputation as a brilliant, provocative lecturer assured large crowds at his courses.

It is on his writings, of course, not on his university activities, that Taylor's fame is based. On one hand, he has produced a number of substantial works of diplomatic history from *The Italian Problem in European Diplomacy* (1934) to *The Origins of the Second World War* (1961), interspersing these with national histories of Germany and the Habsburg Monarchy. All the while Taylor has turned out a steady stream of reviews, special lectures, and essays, and the several published collections of these swell his bibliography to an impressive length. On the other hand, as he once characterized Trevor-Roper, Taylor is himself "anxious—as every great historian must be—to reach a wide audience," and this courting of popularity has led him into the columns of the *Sunday Express* (quite unusual terrain for a respectable British scholar) and onto television panel and lecture programs. On these extracurricular platforms Taylor has released his most mischievous and outrageous pronouncements on both general and specifically historical subjects, disdaining decorous notions of academic propriety for a more congenial role as a sardonic gadfly.

Taylor's double career reflects his two-sided personality. There is, to begin with, no doubt as to the quality of his mind: few other historians can match his broad knowledge of the material of his field, his command of languages, his ability to synthesize a coherent account from a number of diverse sources, and his gift of original insight into the often convention-ridden areas of his concern. At the same time, however, he continually reveals an impish delight in shocking his readers, a delight that often lapses into a cultivated perversity. At bottom he is a dedicated individualist, a scholar devoted to fostering the angularities and oddities in his own personality and in society at large, and to resisting the dulling effect of any kind of orthodoxy or respectability on his cherished orneriness. While Taylor is a proud Englishman, he is an equally proud opponent of the English Establishment, the customary symbol of conformity: "There is nothing more agreeable in life than to make peace with the Establishment," he has written, "and nothing more corrupting;" again, "It is always agreeable to see an arrow being discharged at the great and respectable even if it hits them in the wrong place." Taylor has never found himself at a loss for arrows.

This combination of scholarship and *gaminerie,* then, appears to be what lies behind Taylor's purposes as a historian. Taylor himself has never made any comprehensive statement of why he writes history, or why anyone should write history at all. A reader can only try to piece together a coherent system of values from Taylor's various writings; in doing so, however, he immediately comes up against the barrier posed by Taylor's perversity of style. In his zeal to doubt all received interpretations, Taylor often manages to contradict his own; in straining for the brilliant phrase and the paradoxical epigram, he often obscures whatever serious meaning he might have had. For example, at times he eschews the task of moral judgment in history, or indeed any deeper aim than simple explanation: "I do not believe that a historian should either excuse or condemn. His duty is to explain."

Regarding his own field of diplomatic history, Taylor can suggest outright frivolity: "Nowadays [compared to the period of Ranke] we know better and read diplomatic history for purposes of entertainment." In his more serious moments he declares that the purpose of understanding the past, far from mere amusement, is that "we can come nearer to being, what the men of that time were not, masters of our own destiny." In the same way Taylor takes issue with the notion of amoral technical history and insists that in fact the historian, as a moral being, cannot free himself from moral concerns in writing history. The scholar has a political and social as well as an intellectual existence, and Taylor, turning aside from any pretense of disengagement, reveals his own deep preoccupation with public affairs:

"The historian or the scientist does well to lead a [professionally] dedicated life; yet, however dedicated, he remains primarily a citizen. To turn from political responsibility, to dedication is to open the door to tyranny and measureless barbarism."

What, then, are Taylor's views as a citizen? Here again, because of his self-conscious individualism and provocative style, his position is not easy to characterize. Speaking of himself in the third person, he once wrote, "He believes fanatically in liberty—for himself and others," and in his works there can be found, perhaps as a legacy from his Radical family background, striking traces of Gladstonian-style liberalism. There is no doubt that Taylor is a democrat, with a deep faith in the ultimate wisdom of the people and in the necessity of democratic control of foreign policy. He is at the same time a man of the Left; he has called himself "a life-long socialist; hence has usually been opposed to the policy of the Labour party." But he is nonetheless a supporter of the Campaign for Nuclear Disarmament, and he has been known to make street-corner speeches for Labour candidates in local elections, a pastime not quite so rare among Oxford dons as excursions in the *Sunday Express*.

Thus, with all his perversity and maverick qualities, perhaps because of them, Taylor is a man who takes some things extremely seriously. Often, however, the former traits seem to carry him to the point where he fails to fulfill his own serious purposes. Presumably he accepts the responsibility of teaching through his writings, at least for the sake of his message of personal freedom and moral concern; but then it must be said that his straining after literary effect obscures his own thought and often alienates otherwise sympathetic reader. Taylor indeed falls under his own judgment: "The historian has to combine truth and literary grace; he fails as a historian if he is lacking in either." It has never been easy for Taylor to combine the two, and this as a result of his very brilliance and ingenuity. "We have quite enough clever historians," he once remarked. Yet Taylor himself, as Trevor-Roper complained, "runs the risk of being considered too clever by half."

Turning now to Taylor's works, we can clearly see his major historical concern: nineteenth- and twentieth-century Europe, especially central Europe, and in particular, diplomacy. In all his writings Taylor's Europe is not so much a cultural area or a social entity as a state system, composed of autonomous units maneuvering among one another according to the traditional rules of the Balance of Power. Power indeed is Taylor's theme and his preoccupation, and it is in the changing patterns of the distribution of power (conceived especially in geopolitical terms) that he finds the essential movement of history. It is, moreover, not a random movement; Taylor offers no formulas, but he does assert that there are permanent regularities that determine the course of power relationships:

"Certainly the development of history has its own logical laws. But these laws resemble rather those by which flood-water flows into hitherto unseen channels and forces itself finally to an unpredictable sea."

There are several implications contained in this idea of immanent laws in history. First, theoretically the evolution of the Balance of Power should be inevitable, determined, proceeding on its own way according to history's own logical laws. Indeed Taylor is particularly fond of pointing out automatic consequences inherent in particular historical events or decisions, and he buttresses his analysis with a liberal sprinkling of phrases like "the logic of events," "by an inevitable logic," and so on. On the other hand (and somehow with Taylor there always is the other hand), his narratives move on two levels: the fundamental plane of basic geopolitical forces; and the day-to-day conduct of affairs, depicted through Taylor's masterful handling of a multitude of documentary sources. As he shifts from one level to the other, Taylor leaves as a further implication that the outcome of these determining forces is rarely, if ever, discoverable by the individual statesmen caught up in them; the channels leading to the unpredictable sea are unseen. Thus, the reader is often left with an ambiguous impression: that at each turning-point and decisive stage, the conscious decision and short-range policy of a particular individual profoundly affected the course of history; but also that the decision was made in ignorance of the basic patterns of power, that in fact the statesman made no attempt to think out the long-range consequences of his act; and that in any case his decision and policy could not "logically" have been any different from what they were, given the fundamental forces underlying the whole process.

This conception of history—the Balance of Power working according to inevitable laws—is the intellectual framework into which Taylor places both the results of his historical scholarship and his moral and political values. It is, moreover, the basis not only for his diplomatic history, but for his national history as well. In volumes on Germany and the Habsburg Monarchy Taylor is not concerned with presenting an all-around picture of the development of the life of the country. Rather, he focuses narrowly on its political structure, on the distribution of political power among the various units of the nation—and here political parties, nationalities, and individual political personalities play the same role as the units of the state system in Taylor's diplomatic history. In this way economic, cultural, and social developments are often passed over with a minimum of treatment, unless they seem to Taylor to have some noticeable effect on the power relationships of the major characters of his drama. But it should not be thought that Taylor treats each country as a closed power system, in which a miniature balance works on its own. On the contrary: even in his national histories his concern is always with the European Balance of Power, with the configuration of basic forces on the European scene. Thus, he continually interprets domestic developments as the result of external forces, connecting the power units within each country to the larger, more fundamental geopolitical factors animating European history as a whole.

A few brief examples will serve as illustration. In the case of the Habsburg Monarchy, Taylor depicts a state structure which in its essence was the result of the diplomatic history of Europe, a structure which, once its national-minority units had been set on a course determined by their geographical and political position, was doomed to destruction by the ineluctable operation of historical forces. With little more than a wave of his hand, Taylor is able both to pass over those economic and cultural developments which cannot fit into his schematic interpretation, and to dismiss as inevitably barren all the attempts by Austrian statesmen to find an alternative course.

"The Habsburg Monarchy, more than most Great Powers, was an organization for conducting foreign policy; and its fate was determined quite as much by foreign affairs as by the behavior of its peoples.

. . . Regrets are no part of the duty of a historian, especially when the story which he tells makes clear, time after time, that there were no opportunities to be lost. The conflict between a supernational dynastic state and the national principle had to be fought to the finish; and so, too, had the conflict between the master and subject nations. . . . The national principle, once launched, had to work itself out to its conclusion.

Men thought to alter the European position of the Habsburg Monarchy by changing its internal structure; in reality a change in its internal structure could come only after a change, or rather catastrophe, in its European position.

Thus, all the schemes of the pre-war era postulated the impossible."

Germany, however, affords the most striking example of Taylor's method, and in a sense the entire body of his writings centers around Germany. Taylor's focus in history is on power, and more than with any other state, "the principle which Germany stood for in Europe [was] the principle of military power." *The Course of German History* particularly demonstrates how Taylor can use his conceptual framework to support his personal values of individual freedom as well as to an intense anti-Germanism. To Taylor, Germany's geographical position in Europe, midway between the West and the Slavs of the East led to a permanent condition of artificial, impermanent frontiers, and so to a Germany never fully Western and liberal, and never reconciled to living peacefully with her Slav neighbors. As a consequence the Germans were never able to concentrate on winning freedom for themselves within Germany; surrendering to absolutism, "they strengthened the military monarchy and urged it on to conquer others in order to console themselves for the fact that they had been themselves conquered." Further, since this "German problem" was the result of a permanent situation in the European Balance of Power, the German national character resulting from it was equally permanent—"for more than a thousand years . . . recognizably the same"—brutal, aggressive, aping the traditions of the West, and turning Western technical achievements to the service of barbarism. Thus the Germans could do nothing to rescue themselves; only a change in the original external situation, that is, interference by other European states, could change the configuration of power and bring peace and democracy to Germany.

In all this, Taylor is not simply presenting a detached explanation of German development. As he urged others to do, he himself is writing not only as a historian but as a citizen; despite his disclaimers in the Preface, he is in fact suggesting his own political remedies to the "German problem." The essential requirement, based on Taylor's conception of the operation of the Balance of Power, is European cooperation to keep Germany in check. The absence of this cooperation allowed Bismarck to triumph in 1870. This cooperation, albeit imperfect, imposed the Versailles Treaty, "the only security for German democracy, or for German Christian civilization;" its breakdown left the Germans to their own devices, that is, to Nazism, and only the renewal of European solidarity, "by the greatest act of statesmanship of the century—say rather, of modern times" (Churchill's alliance with Russia in 1941), made it possible to choke off the latest and worst bout of German aggressiveness. And the implications for today? In a climactic statement reflecting both his politics and his historiography, Taylor does not shrink from his conclusion:

"How can we build up Germany as a Great Power and use her as an ally against the Soviet Union without risk to ourselves? The answer is simple: it is not possible, and those who attempt the impossible will sooner or later pay the price. Preserving the present situation is the kindest policy towards the Germans themselves. For only a divided Germany can be a free Germany. A reunited Germany would cease to be free—either it would become a militaristic state in order to resume the march towards European domination, or its power would be compulsorily reduced by foreign interference, if the former allies had the sense to come together in time."

Is *The Course of German History,* in which both Taylor's political views and his conception of the geopolitical Balance of Power figure so prominently, a typical product of his historiography? It can be pointed out on one side that he completed the manuscript in 1944 and first published it in England in 1945, when revulsion against Germany was at its height. Yet Taylor allowed the work to be republished in 1962 with only minor corrections, restating his earlier conclusions in a new Preface, as he had previously done in many of his reviews and essays. When we turn to his major works of diplomatic history, however, the picture changes: the profound factors of power relationships, as well as political overtones, seem at first sight less significant than before, and we are plunged into an almost day-by-day account of diplomatic correspondence and the comings and goings of ambassadors and cabinet ministers.

It has been suggested that in this respect Taylor is an exemplar of "pure" diplomatic history—that is, the account of relations between governments (that is, between their foreign ministries), drawn chiefly, if not exclusively, from diplomatic archives supplemented perhaps by the memoirs of statesmen—as it was once put, "what one clerk said to another clerk." This is a narrow conception of history, ignoring the deeper social and economic forces behind the foreign policies reflected in the formal documents, and neglecting also some of the deeper power factors present in Taylor's German work. In attempting to answer the question of whether or not Taylor is a "pure" diplomatic historian, once again we find an ambiguous answer. If we look at his professions, he seems not to be; if we look at his practice, apparently he is.

In his essays there are some examples of indecision on this point. Apart from them, perhaps the most flagrant contradiction occurs in *The Struggle for Mastery in Europe,* where two divergent viewpoints are neatly sandwiched within a single book. The first chapter, on one hand, is an impressive analysis of the economic and military bases of power in the European states from 1848 to 1918, and of the effect of these factors in the evolution of the international Balance of Power during that period. Again, in the bibliographical essay at the end of the volume Taylor makes a great deal of the growing force of public opinion (as he does from time to time in the text), and in fact there can be found, buried deep in the essay, the statement: "Policy springs from deep social and economic sources; it is not crudely manufactured in foreign offices." The rest of the book, however, might just as well have been written without these pregnant suggestions. Economic considerations intrude only slightly and infrequently (and, as it happens, unconvincingly). We are seldom given a clear picture of public opinion; in any case, we are never told of Taylor's sources for it, despite his frequent assertions of its importance. Nowhere in the book, finally, is there a discussion of the social, economic, and psychological forces behind such a phenomenon as the rise of imperialism; such a treatment is beyond the narrow range of Taylor's documentary sources.

To a high degree the book displays Taylor's real merits—his command of the voluminous diplomatic sources, and his ability to synthesize them and arrive at many original and thought-provoking, if paradoxically expressed and occasionally contradictory, interpretations. Nor is there a complete break with his earlier method. Rather, Taylor here takes for granted the basic impulses of German aggressiveness and Habsburg difficulties which are the themes of his earlier works; they underlie the closely followed diplomatic account, even though they seldom come to the surface. It is true that Taylor has somewhat softened several of his earlier damning judgments of Germany, but his essential conclusion is a familiar one: that the inevitable failure of Austria-Hungary to solve her national problems, together with Germany's typical attempt to subdue the Continent, brought on the war. Behind it all lay the unalterable character of the German people. In a sentence that might have come out of his wartime manuscript, Taylor declares:

"In fact, peace must have brought Germany the mastery of Europe within a few years. This was prevented by the habit of her diplomacy and, still more, by the mental outlook of her people. They had trained themselves psychologically for aggression."

There ensued the destruction of the European Balance, which had existed self-sufficiently until then, the rise of two Great Powers on the fringe of Europe (Soviet Russia and the United States), and the sad but inevitable outcome—"what had been the centre of the world became merely 'the European question.'"

Thus far, whether it be in terms of the fundamental elements of geopolitics or the day-to-day conduct of diplomacy, the Germans to Taylor have always remained an inevitably disturbing, aggressive force bent on overthrowing the European Balance of Power. It is Taylor's most recent scholarly work, *The Origins of the Second World War*, that has made his readers and colleagues wonder if the staunch anti-Germanist has performed a *volte-face* and set out to rehabilitate the Germans in general and Hitler in particular. In truth, there are contradictions between this and earlier books which simply cannot be reconciled, but it is equally true that both the broad conceptions and the political implications in this work are generally consistent with what Taylor has written for many years.

The thesis of the book and the major criticisms of it (by Trevor-Roper and others) are by now so well known that they need be summarized only briefly. In a word, Taylor's analysis of the origins of the war centers on his interpretation of Hitler—not a demonic Führer with far-ranging schemes for a New Order in Europe, but (as he put it elsewhere) simply "the ordinary German writ large," with only limited aims, with perhaps no ideas of his own at all, but with an uncanny ability to profit opportunistically from the blunders of Britain and France. Those blunders, indeed, brought on the war—blunders by which the Western powers either surrendered to Hitler unnecessarily, or which provoked him unnecessarily into a European conflict. In Taylor's now notorious words, "The war of 1939, far from being premeditated, was a mistake, the result on both sides of diplomatic blunders."

In the process of demonstrating this thesis Taylor has been

guilty of two serious failures, a failure of conception and a failure of responsibility. In the first place, he has approached the diplomatic history of the interwar period in much the same way as he did that of the pre-1914 years, through official diplomatic documents and occasional memoirs. But for the later period that method is even less adequate than it had been for the earlier age. The nub of Taylor's interpretation is his notion of German policy; the determining factor of German policy was Hitler, and Hitler's policy cannot be reconstructed from the diplomatic documents alone. Its dynamism, its open-ended expansionism, its far-reaching conceptions (ranging from annexation of Austria to a continent-wide racial policy)—all these elements Taylor has omitted. By reducing all activism in German policy to the lowest point possible, Taylor has paradoxically reversed the ordinary chain of causal explanation. Hitler's bold enterprises have become simply reactions to British and French moves; and what were in part their responses to positive German steps have been transformed into active initiatives which dropped concessions into Hitler's lap—an interpretation which a wider conceptual framework and a more generous use of such sources as *Mein Kampf* would make untenable.

What is worse, and here the question of responsibility enters, even the material which Taylor has used will not bear his thesis without considerable distortion and strained interpretation. There are on one hand inaccuracies in quotation from the documents, and a tendency to dismiss as "play-acting" Hitler's statements (such as his military plans) not consistent with Taylor's thesis. At the same time Taylor can be guilty of outrageous frivolity: to say airily that "in his first years of power, Hitler did not concern himself much with foreign affairs" is to ignore the overwhelming weight of evidence in the diplomatic documents themselves—an instance of the consequences of Taylor's excessive cleverness.

As for the matter of consistency, it is an exacting task indeed to sort out Taylor's contradictions. Within this single volume he can dismiss *Mein Kampf* as a useful key to Hitler's plans, and then use it himself; he can emphasize the achievements of American policy in the 1920's, and then sneer that no one missed America's absence; he can insist that Hitler's policy is capable of rational explanation, and then explain it by Hitler's sixth sense. Once Taylor's earlier works are added to the picture, inconsistencies with his later opinions appear and are impossible to resolve, whether they concern Hitler's intentions toward Czechoslovakia, his evil and visionary policies, or his nature as "a titanic demon."

There are, nevertheless, striking points of agreement connecting *Origins* with Taylor's other writings, among them a political theme which is much less blatant here than in his German history, but which is no less important and perhaps not so very different. Let us, to begin with, take Taylor's thesis at face value; what were the Allied blunders which led to war: They were, first, unnecessarily anticipating and imagining long-range German threats where none existed (as with Czechoslovakia in March, 1939, or Poland later in that year); second, divorcing morality from considerations of power (as the British did first at Munich and again with the Polish guarantee); third, treating Europe as a closed system by neglecting Russia and America, and so attempting to resurrect the defunct European Balance of Power which had collapsed by 1918. It was the essence of that Balance, as Taylor repeats in his earlier works and implies here, that a Europe which fails to unite against a unified Germany is going to fall under German domination—peacefully, if German policy is sane and patient, by war, if it is not.

Even in *Origins,* with all his emphasis on the day-to-day course of diplomacy, Taylor does not neglect the basic forces animating his earlier narratives. Once again, he writes on two levels: the first and more prominent one, that of conventional diplomacy, on which accidents and blunders can indeed cause a world war; the second and only occasionally apparent level, that of geopolitical realities, on which the war was practically inevitable. It was so because Germany as a result of the Armistice and the Peace had been allowed to remain unified; and it was the dominance of a unified Germany in a Europe from which Russia and America were effectively absent that was the "natural order of things" with which, in Taylor's view, Munich complied, and which, given the configuration of power, was irresistible. The only thing that could have prevented the inevitable outcome was the intervention of Russia and America in European affairs. Such an intervention would have set up a new Balance of Power to restrain

Germany and, by furthering separatist movements within Germany, would have ensured German democracy and European peace.

Now what does this thesis of Taylor the historian have to do with the views of Taylor the politically concerned citizen? The implications of Taylor's history for politics today do not lead to simple appeasement of Russia, as Trevor-Roper has suggested. While Taylor does assert that "if I had to choose, I'd rather be anti-German and pro-Russian than the other way round," still he can hardly be called pro-Communist. As far as relations with Germany are concerned, Taylor's message is still the same: if we recreate a united Germany and use it to exclude Russia from Europe, we shall ipso facto re-create the conditions of the inter-war period and bring either German dominion of Europe or another world war. What is required to prevent this is the same factor that was missing in 1870 and between the wars, and that Churchill restored in 1941—European unity against Germany. Regarding our relations with Russia, we must avoid making the same errors analyzed in *Origins*: looking for long-range schemes of Russian aggression where none exist, for according to Taylor, Russian policy is still based on fear of Germany; judging Russian action on grounds of "whole-hogging morality;" blundering unnecessarily into war, as almost happened in Korea.

Behind all this, finally, is Taylor's deep anxiety for individual liberty. The consequence of present diplomacy that he fears most is the division of Europe and the world as a whole into two rigid and hostile camps, one based on Russia, the other on America, for neither can give Europe what Taylor most values: "To the present day, the one Great Power offers Europe repression, the other material wealth. Neither can offer liberty of spirit which was the true aim of 1848." Thus Taylor has opposed the Common Market and Britain's entry into it as steps that would only harden the present dualism in Europe. Again, for the sake of liberty of spirit it is the part of the Western nations to resist the overwhelming weight of American influence, always tending to press the allies into a mold of cultural mediocrity and a barren and inflexible anti-Russianism. To Taylor the practical implication is clear: Britain must regain her freedom of choice in diplomacy (still a real possibility in his opinion), and then lead the way to a gradual loosening-up of the two great power blocs. There is already a beginning for Britain to follow: "The best thing for us and for the world in general is that we should be America's Tito."

Here perhaps is the point where Taylor's politics, his temperament, and his historical conceptions converge. For the role Taylor assigns to Britain is the one he has so often played himself: the gadfly, the constant critic of the respectable and the powerful, the individualist outside of conventional groupings who pricks the pretensions of the orthodox and "believes fanatically in liberty—for himself and others." At the same time Taylor's foreign policy, if it reveals a cultivated perversity, also shows considerable intellectual elaboration. It is the outcome of an immense historical learning and of an insight into the operation of European politics, both the products of a brilliant historical mind.

The question remains, what importance does Taylor have for practicing historians and students of history? Approaching him as a man, we must acknowledge the quality of his intellect and, as well, his public-spirited engagement with what he considers the most pressing issues of public policy. Approaching him as a historian, we cannot help but be instructed by his brilliant syntheses and his original insights, even when they are wrong or wrongheaded. At this point, however, a nagging reservation must be faced: does Taylor have the imposing greatness or the strength of personality to redeem his errors, as do unquestionably great historians, like Macaulay or Namier? Answering tentatively and on the basis of his publicly apparent character, it is difficult to say so. Too often Taylor's proud individualism seems reduced to perversity and orneriness for their own sake, not for the sake of either a grand historical vision or an ennobling personal mission; too often those ideals of which are appealing seem obscured and compromised by the very character that produced them. Taylor's lesson for us remains in the end a warning against the temptations of brilliance, an admonition not to take one's intellectual gifts too lightly—or perhaps too seriously.

Mr. Taylor's Reply

Magdalen College,
Oxford.

21 xi 64.

Dear Mr. Segel,

It is not for me to criticise your article which I enjoyed and much appreciated. I'm sorry you did not mention *The Trouble-makers,* my favourite book and, I think, my best. Otherwise no complaints. As to message or meaning in my work, you'll find all I have to say on that subject in the first few lines of the preface to *Englishmen and Others.* I have a blank spot in my mind about such things—it's like being colourblind. Same with profound forces and general trends. Other historians use these concepts, and no doubt they are right—we should never get through the stuff otherwise. I'm just not good at it. That is why I cover them always in a few pages and then go over to detail which I am better at.

I have no delight, impish or otherwise, in shocking readers. I don't care one way or the other. I put down what seems to me right without worrying whether it is orthodox or shocking. Readers who insist on being shocked have only themselves to blame. I am only shocked by bad scholarship. And of course if I wanted notoriety (which I don't particularly) I have much easier ways of attaining it than by twisting history.

You complain of inconsistencies in my books. Some no doubt exist. Usually they are due to having learnt better. I often start by taking a current or accepted view for granted, and then on detailed examination find that it doesn't work. This happened with the *Origins of the Second World War.* I had no idea at the beginning how it would work out. Gradually I discovered how dated and misleading most of the books were. They assumed from the start that Hitler was responsible for it all. I assumed nothing one way or the other. This is what shocked people— particularly for some reason Americans. I don't understand why American historians wrote such offensive reviews, full of personal abuse. Vested interests? Intolerance? Or is there something in

SOURCE. Personal letter published by permission of the author.

my writing peculiarly provoking to Americans? You must explain it to me.

To me, you see, Hitler is dead and the war of 1939, like everything else concerned with him, is a matter of detached historical curiosity. If I were to return the abuse, I could say—to Sontag for example—that I was plugging for war against Germany long before 1939 and that my country declared war on its own choice. Citizens of a country which only got into the war when Hitler condescended to declare war on it are not entitled to reproach anyone except themselves.

Most of the stories about Hitler have turned out to be myths. The Reichstag fire as a Nazi plot is now a dead dog, abandoned even by the Germans, as Krausnick recently admitted to me. Massive German rearmament is a myth—no proper economic mobilisation until February 1942. I've only gone a bit further and shown that Hitler had no detailed plans or schemes for world conquest. He was a dynamic force on the make. At any rate I think Hitler's wickedness has to be proved, not assumed.

I try to write without thinking that I'm English or a radical or a socialist. You'll be able to judge how far I have succeeded when my *English History 1914–1915* comes out. One of my colleagues complained that it was too patriotic.

Yours sincerely,

A. J. P. Taylor

2   *A Memorandum from Adolf Hitler*
            to Professor A. J. P. Taylor

Horizon's *editorials by William Harlan Hale often deal*
vitriolically with controversial topics.

I have received from below a copy of your book *The Origins*
of the Second World War, newly published and widely discussed
in several nations of the West. Up here it is usually twilight,
and I am not reading much. Thereby I avoid tiring my eyes
with the slanders of history-scribblers about my late earthly Mission. But your book is *different.* So different, Herr Professor, that
I am pleased to extend you congratulations upon it. It tells not
all the truth, but enough of the truth to reverse the recent tendency below to propagate the Lie.

I am glad to recognize, also, that the author is a distinguished
professor at a University for which I have held the highest senti-
ments; did I not repeatedly tell that rascal Goering not to bomb
it? Your Work—and I trust it is only the first of many that will
find the right direction—proves to me the reawakening good sense
of scholars in the West.

Your text, written in admirably clear English, reviews the whole
history of Europe between the two wars and specifically absolves
me of guilt for the second. Thus you write, "The peace of Versailles lacked moral validity from the start." Right! Precisely what
I said from my own start. You declare that all I set out to do was
to recover for Germany the "natural" place in Europe of which
she had been deprived by Versailles. I could not have said it
better myself. You show, correctly, that the Austrian crisis of 1938,
which unfortunately forced me to take over that country, was
precipitated not by me but by the Austrians themselves, and that
"it was sprung on him [Hitler] by surprise." Next you prove that
the Czech crisis that followed it was actually "of British making,"

not of mine. Finally you demonstrate beyond a doubt that when Poland's turn came in the following year, my objective was simply friendly "alliance with Poland, not her destruction." Right, three times right!!!

You sum up that "Hitler did not make plans—for world conquest or for anything else." Here I must take exception, Herr Professor. Surely, you must grant that I made at least *some* plans! I was a statesman, not an idiot! But I agree entirely when you observe that "the state of German armament in 1939 gives the decisive proof that Hitler was not contemplating general war, and probably not intending war at all." How well you comprehend my situation then: with my thin line of Panzers, my still-raw recruits, and my wavering generals, how could I have possibly thought of aggression? Then I *would* have been an idiot!

I am grateful for so full a vindication, particularly when it comes from one formerly in the enemy camp. Clearly, I owe it to the English sense of fair play. Once before, after Versailles, many decent elements in both England and America showed similar insight, and absolved my predecessor, William II, from all but just a little guilt. In my case, since I had been accused of so much more, your problem must have been greater, yet how completely you have overcome it, and how soon. One can always rely on an Anglo-Saxon gentleman's broadmindedness and his willingness to make amends.

For amends there must be. If I did not aggress, Herr Professor, then who did? Surely someone did! I think you have already provided the way to the answer. You write, for instance, that "the second World war grew out of the victories in the first." Rarely has a master of the historian's art expressed so much in so few words! For they can only mean that the Allied victors in the first war were themselves responsible for the second. And later you make yourself even clearer when you applaud the Munich settlement which your Mr. Chamberlain made with me by calling it "a triumph for all that was best and most enlightened in British life." Indeed it was! From this it must follow that those elements that repudiated Munich—your war-leaders, in short—represented the very opposite: all that was worst and least enlightened in British life. If Chamberlain and I were right, who was wrong? Since you correctly declare that I did not start the war, those who started it were evidently . . .

But I hardly need say the final word. From your own pages the conclusion all but leaps to the eye of anyone who can read English.

3 *The Exchange in* The Times Literary Supplement

The Times Literary Supplement *is, perhaps, the most highly respected English review. The review articles always appear anonymously, but authors of letters to the Editor are identified. Among the prominent scholars who participated in the debate about the* Origins *are the late David Thomson, Master of Sidney Sussex College of Cambridge University and the prolific author of general histories; Isaac Deutscher, the historian of Russia and biographer of Trotsky; Margaret Lambert, an Editor of the* Documents on British Foreign Policy; *W. N. Medlicott, Professor Emeritus of Diplomatic History at the London School of Economics*; Georges Bonnin, a specialist of Hitler's rise to power; Elizabeth Wiskemann, an anti-fascist writer of long experience; A. L. Rowse, the historian of Elizabethan England; and H. R. Trevor-Roper, the Regius Professor of Modern History at Oxford University.*

April 21, 1961

"WHY DID WE FIGHT"

(*Anonymous*)

The origins of the Second World War, unlike those of the first, have been more or less taken for granted. The verdict of Nuremberg is still the common opinion of most historians: that the war happened because Hitler and his henchmen willed it. The explanation, as Mr. Taylor points out, has suited almost everybody.

SOURCE. The Exchange in *The Times Literary Supplement* is reprinted by special permission of the Times Literary Supplement and the scholars who participated in this Debate.

* Professor Medlicott declined to have his letter republished, but his views appear below, pp. 94–96.

It has suited the western allies because it covers up their own deficiencies of policy; it has suited Hitler's allies because it partially exonerates them; and it has suited the German people because, although the most honest of them do not deny their guilt for many aspects of Nazism, they can at least acquit themselves of being congenital and incorrigible war-mongers. But it has not suited Mr. Taylor, who has applied his brilliant gifts to demolishing what he conceives to be a myth. The exercise is simple, devastating, superlatively readable, and deeply disturbing.

It is disturbing because it does to Nuremberg what inter-war German propaganda tried to do to Versailles. Mr. Taylor indeed admits that the Treaty of Versailles "lacked moral validity from the start." He will perhaps not be surprised if future German historians say the same thing about the trials at Nuremberg, and quote him in support; but many of his admirers will be surprised at such an outcome, for they know him as not by any means the most Germanophile of historians. That is not to say that they will cease to be his admirers, if they are honest with themselves, for the cogency of his analysis is indisputable. Paragraph after paragraph and page after page build up with methodical and impeccable logic to an apparently irresistible conclusion that Hitler, so far from having planned a world war all along, became involved in it in 1939 "through launching on 29 August a diplomatic manoeuvre which he ought to have launched on 28 August." In one sentence, "the war of 1939, far from being premeditated, was a mistake, the result on both sides of diplomatic blunders."

To follow Mr. Taylor's argument in detail would require an inordinately long review. It must clearly be submitted to critical examination, as it no doubt will be by English historians who are named as architects of the myth which he seeks to destroy. On first inspection it can only be said that Mr. Taylor's work looks likely to stand up successfully to examination as close and detached as he has given to his sources. As with most of his historical writing, one is left wondering at the perversity which has prevented any university institution in the country from giving a professorial chair to one of England's two or three outstanding historians. But inevitably the wonder is discoloured by occasional reflections on Mr. Taylor's own perversity, of which there are some (fortunately fewer than usual) examples in his new book. One not unimportant example may be taken as typical.

He refers in the summer of 1939 to "a member of the Foreign
Office who was sent to Moscow for some obscure purpose." This
was in fact Mr. William (now Lord) Strang, and the purpose of
his mission was the subject of a public statement by the Prime
Minister of the day. Mr. Taylor might perhaps consider himself
justified in a cynical retort that the obscurity was not thereby re-
lieved. But the episode is also the subject of a full account in
Lord Strang's autobiography, *Home and Abroad,* which finally
dispels the various misinterpretations current at the time. Turning to Mr. Taylor's rather imperfect bibliography, one finds him
saying that "I failed to derive anything useful from the writings
of (among others) Strang." It must indeed be agreed that this
was a failure on his part, though that does not seem to be the
intention of his presumably sarcastic reference.

Mr. Taylor still damages his reputation by clinging too long
to his position as the top "angry young man" of historical scholarship. But although occasional irritation may overshadow judgment, it should not be allowed to detract from admiration of a
startlingly brilliant performance. Whether or not his judgment
stands permanently, this is the first time that we have been able
to read an account of the inter-war period which is the work of
a scholar studying history rather than the commentary of a contemporary reliving a part of his own experience.

[The following letters from prominent English scholars subse-
quently appeared in *The Times Literary Supplement.*]

May 5, 1961

Sir,—Your reviewer of Mr. A. J. P. Taylor's *The Origins of the
Second World War* . . . by refraining from giving examples of the
book's "methodical and impeccable logic" does less than justice
to the author's remarkable gifts. A handful of such examples may
help.

In 1918, we are told, "Russia disappeared from view—her
revolutionary government, her very existence, ignored by the
victorious Powers." But fifteen pages later we are reminded,
quite correctly, that "The Western Powers had entangled themselves in wars of intervention against Bolshevik rule even while
the war against Germany was still on: then they encouraged the

cordon sanitaire of states on Russia's western border: finally they resigned themselves to a policy of non-recognition. . . ."

Mr. Taylor points out that "The Anglo-French entente and the Eastern alliance did not supplement each other; they cancelled out," and adds that this deadlock "existed implicitly from the first moment, and no one, either British or French, ever found a way round it." But [later] the Locarno agreements mean that France's "two contradictory systems of diplomacy were reconciled, at any rate on paper."

It seems that France in the mid-thirties "had no forces capable of intervention" though "even in 1939 the German army was not equipped for a prolonged war; and in 1940 the German land forces were inferior to the French in everything except leadership."

It is interesting to be told that Hitler's reoccupation of the Rhineland led to Belgium's withdrawal from the French alliance which "created a terrible strategical problem for the French," since it left France's Belgian border without defences. It is a trifle puzzling, however, when we have been assured that "The reoccupation of the Rhineland did not affect France from the defensive point of view."

So, too, with Hitler's aims. "Whatever his long-term plans (and it is doubtful whether he had any), the mainspring of his immediate policy had been 'the destruction of Versailles.' " Two pages later, "Hitler intended to make Germany the leading Power in Europe, with Italy as, at best, a junior partner."

Such gifts of ventriloquism, being rare among historians, surely deserve some comment?

DAVID THOMSON

Sidney Sussex College, Cambridge

Sir,—Mr. Taylor will not need any help from me in defending himself against Dr. Thomson's criticisms (May 5). But I should like to point out on my own behalf the futility of trying to give examples of a "methodical and impeccable logic" which runs through the whole of a long and closely woven argument. It is only the occasional lapse from logic that can be so illustrated; and that is what Dr. Thomson has done. He had not, however, in my opinion, significantly impaired, or even touched, the main structure of Mr. Taylor's argument. I am sorry that he has not, because it would have been a relief to me if he had been able to do so.

YOUR REVIEWER

June 2, 1961

Sir,—May I join in the discussion about your review of Mr. A. J. P. Taylor's book with a brief remark? I first became acquainted with Mr. Taylor's work by reading his *Course of German History*, published in 1945. That book was an epitome of war-time "Vansittartism." Its moral was that not only did the Germans bear exclusive responsibility for the Second World War, but that *all* Germans, anti-Nazis as well as Nazis, were guilty. The moral of his latest book is that *no* German, not even Hitler, was really guilty. Neither of these simplifications has anything in common with historical scholarship. Mr. Taylor poses as an "unorthodox" and "radical" historian. Yet in each of these two books he has only provided a pseudo-academic justification for a prevalent trend of official policy: the *Course of German History* justified the policies of Yalta and Potsdam, "unconditional surrender," and the plans which were then *en vogue* for the dismemberment and de-industrialization of Germany; and the *Origins of the Second World War* is in striking harmony with the mood which is now dominant and favours the Western alliance with Germany and Germany's rearmament. Your reviewer speaks of Mr. Taylor's "impeccable logic;" but is this not the logic of a truly Orwellesque "re-write" of history?

ISAAC DEUTSCHER

Sir,—Your reviewer is unable to see the flaw in Mr. Taylor's argument that Hitler did not plan the Second World War. The flaw is very simple. Mr. Taylor lays down that: "In my opinion statesmen are too absorbed by events to follow a preconceived plan." Then whenever the records show Hitler expounding his preconceived plan Mr. Taylor merely denies that Hitler meant what he said. A good illustration of Mr. Taylor's method occurs [when] he is discussing the so-called Hossbach memorandum, which consists of notes made by Hitler's adjutant of Hitler's exposition of his foreign policy given in a secret conference in the Reich Chancellery, on November 5, 1937. The conference was attended, besides Hossbach, only by Blomberg, Hitler's War Minister, Neurath, his Foreign Minister, and his three services chiefs, Fritsch, Raeder and Goering. Hitler began by stressing the extreme importance and secrecy of his exposition and "asked in the interests of a long-term German foreign policy that his exposition should be regarded in the event of his death as his last will and testament."

Mr. Taylor omits these words. Instead he makes light of the conference: "Hitler did most of the talking. He began with a general disquisition on Germany's need for *Lebensraum*." In the actual momorandum of the conference Hitler is recorded as having said: "Germany's problem could only be solved by means of force [*Gewalt*] and this was never without attendant risk. The campaigns [*Kämpfe*] of Frederick the Great for Silesia and Bismarck's wars [*Kriege*] against Austria and France had involved unheard-of risks, and the swiftness of the Prussian action in 1870 had kept Austria from entering the war." It is therefore perfectly clear that Hitler was talking about war. Mr. Taylor, having omitted the second sentence of this passage, tries to argue as follows: "He [Hitler] went on to demonstrate that Germany would gain her aims without a great war; *'force' apparently meant to him the threat of war, not war itself*." (Italics mine.) This is mere quibbling. Did "force" apparently mean to Frederick the Great "the threat of war, not war itself?" Further on, when setting the time for action as, at the very latest, 1943–45, Hitler said: "Zudem erwarte die Welt unseren Schlag und treffe ihre Gegenmassnahmen von Jahr zu Jahr mehr. Während die Umwelt sich abriegele, seien wir zur Offensive gezwungen." ("In addition the world was awaiting our blow and was taking increasing countermeasures from year to year. It was whilst the rest of the world was still preparing its defences [*lit.* barring itself off] that we were compelled to take the offensive.") Nothing could be clearer than that and naturally Mr. Taylor does not quote it. Instead he announces that "Hitler's exposition was mere day-dreaming unrelated to what happened in real life," an assertion for which he can produce no evidence, merely his own speculation.

As for Mr. Taylor's further piece of speculation, that: "There was no crisis in foreign policy. The conference was a mere manoeuvre in domestic affairs," because "Hitler feared Schacht and could not answer his financial arguments", there is evidence in the opposite sense. Hitler had already dealt with those arguments. He did so in a memorandum written in the summer of 1936, of which the text may most conveniently be found in the *Viertel-jahrshefte für Zeitgeschichte*, 1955, No. 2, since it is not printed in the Major War Criminals at Nuremberg (it was Defence Exhibit: Schacht: No. 48); an English translation is to be found in Case XI of the subsequent proceedings.

MARGARET LAMBERT

Sir,—It is difficult to understand the strong reactions evoked by Mr. Taylor's thesis that Hitler had not planned a world war. For those who are familiar with the German diplomatic documents, this has been a known fact for many years. Indeed, in spite of the contrary opinion of your reviewer, one can read Mr. Taylor's thesis in the judgment of the Nuremberg Military Tribunal: the Nazi leaders were not condemned for planning a European war, let alone a world war; they were found guilty of a war of aggression against Poland.

Perhaps even more important, American inquiries after the war revealed that, in spite of a great show of rearmament and military power, Nazi Germany was not prepared for a war on any large scale.

The debate initiated by Mr. Taylor is, of course, not a moral one, but, within its limits, it is difficult to see how Mr. Taylor can be criticized.

GEORGES BONNIN
St. Antony's College, Oxford

Sir,—On April 22 the *Reichsruf*, the organ of the neo-Nazi *Reichspartei* in the Federal Republic, jubilantly welcomed Mr. Taylor's mis-reading of the Hossbach Memorandum and attacked German historians who had read it with greater care. The *Deutsche Soldatenzeitung* of April 28 was happy to note that Mr. Taylor had made nonsense of the Nuremberg trials. The May number of *Nation-Europa* (published in Coburg by Artur Ehrhardt, formerly a Major in the S.S., on behalf of the chief neo-Nazi international organization) was gratified to observe that Mr. Taylor had explained away the responsibility of Nazi Germany for the Second World War. Sir Oswald Mosley's *Action* has expressed similar appreciation of Mr. Taylor.

ELIZABETH WISKEMANN

May 26, 1961

Sir,—Dr. David Thomson is not alone in observing the utter failure of your reviewer to diagnose what is the case with Mr. A. J. P. Taylor's astonishing and deplorable reconstruction of the events leading to the war, and the presentation of it *as history*. It is, indeed, a serious matter for the good name of English historical writing as well as for its effects upon the public.

Dr. Thomson adduces a series of flagrant self-contradictions from the book. And there are many others. Let us take only one example—the author's treatment of the Munich crisis.

We are told that "the Czechoslovak problem was not of British making; the Czech crisis of 1938 was." Only two pages before we are given the Sudeten leader, Henlein's, own words, "We must always demand so much that we can never be satisfied." But one page before we learn that "the crisis over Czechoslovakia was provided for Hitler. He merely took advantage of it." But [later] this is contradicted: "The Sudeten leaders, true to their instructions from Hitler, always kept a demand ahead, and tantalized Runciman as they had tantalized Benes."

What are we to make of this mass of self-contradictions? Any responsible historian should be ashamed of them. This irresponsibility about the truth of the matter is the ultimate offence for an historian, whose business is to care for the truth more than anything.

In fact, the public is presented with an inversion of common sense and truth. The Czechoslovak crisis was *not* created by the British Government, as we all know; it was created and continually stepped up by Hitler. Your reviewer disarmingly asks for guidance on the general question, and it is important that responsibly minded historians should give it, in the public interest.

Mr. A. J. P. Taylor tells us that "in principle and doctrine, Hitler was no more wicked and unscrupulous than many other contemporary statesmen. In wicked acts he outdid them all." This is a completely false disjunction. If a man believes the wicked rub-bush of anti-Semitism, teaches it, inculcates it, enforces it, it leads straight to the racial murders that Hitler perpetrated.

One would have thought that the moral sensibility of a prominent unilateral disarmer would have been aware of this crux. But there is self-contradiction in the moral choices and judgments as in the presentation of the facts. Throughout the book, Mr. A. J. P. Taylor is at pains to whittle down moral considerations, to insinuate that everybody was equally more or less to blame, until there appears little difference between those who inculcated and practised race-murder and those who did not.

There is a very important difference between those who commit and those who do not. However poor our opinion may be of British statesmen in the 1930s, they were not murderers; Hitler and the Nazi leaders were. It is a disgrace to have to remind Mr. A. J. P. Taylor of this difference—there is little to remind us in his book, where everything is reduced to much the same level of muchness.

On the last page of the book we are told—another contradiction: "Hitler may have projected a great war all along; yet it seems from the record that he became involved in war through launching on 29 August a diplomatic manoeuvre which he ought to have launched on 28 August."

There are scholars I know who describe all this, appropriately enough, as through-the-looking-glass history. But when I consider the issues involved, of historical truth and presentation, of the deep responsibility of the historian to the public to get things right and state them scrupulously, as against this fundamental frivolity, I can only describe it as intellectually deplorable.

A. L. ROWSE

Sir,—Your reviewer, having referred explicitly to Mr. Taylor's "methodical and impeccable logic," now declares that it would be "futile" to illustrate such logic; it is only possible to illustrate "occasional lapses from logic," and such lapses, if they occur, do not "significantly impair or even touch" "the main structure" of any argument which he has once declared impeccable. Would your reviewer now come out into the open and say clearly (1) what he means by "impeccable;" (2) what he means by "logic;" (3) how he distinguishes peccable from impeccable logic?

H. R. TREVOR-ROPER

Our Reviewer writes:—By "impeccable" I mean without flaws; by "logic" I mean a chain of reasoning. I have never used the word "peccable," but I take it that the distinction Professor Trevor-Roper has in mind is between a faulty and a correct chain of reasoning. As an example of a faulty one, I would refer to the last part of his first sentence, which states neither what I argued nor anything that follows necessarily from it.

The sentence in my review which referred to Mr. Taylor's logic was concerned with the question whether or not Hitler planned the Second World War. I have not yet seen any flaw revealed in Mr. Taylor's argument that he did not. Dr. Rowse's letter, impressive though his indignation is, does not deal with that point. I must leave it to Mr. Taylor to meet the general criticisms of his book, which as I said in my review of it, were bound to be made.

Mr. Taylor replied abruptly to the entire correspondence:

Sir,—I have no sympathy with authors who resent criticism or try to answer it. I must however thank your correspondents for the free publicity which they have given to my book.

A. J. P. TAYLOR
Magdalen College, Oxford

4   *Elizabeth Wiskemann*
                   in The Listener

*Elizabeth Wiskemann is a professional writer who specializes
on European history in the fascist era. Her works include* The
Rome-Berlin Axis: A History of the Relations between Hitler
and Mussolini *(New York, 1949), and* Europe of the Dictators,
1919–1945 *(New York, 1966).*

Mr. Taylor has produced an intensely readable analysis of the
events leading to the war of 1939 as he chooses to present them.
His ability to quote from diplomatic documents without getting
bogged down in them, as others do, is masterly. His main proposition is stated on page 216. "The blame for war can be put on
Hitler's Nihilism instead of on the faults and failures of European statesmen—faults and failures which their public shared.
Human blunders, however, usually do more to shape history than
human wickedness. At any rate this is a rival dogma which is
worth developing, if only as an academic exercise." Mr. Taylor
certainly performs very skilful gymnastics, but it is a little doubtful whether his exercise remains academic. Those whom he
brands as misled by their eagerness to cry opprobrium never be-
littled the blunders as Mr. Taylor belittles the wickedness; indeed
the blunders seemed greater against the background of the programme which is now denied to the innocent Hitler.

It is amusing to observe Mr. Taylor's use of the evidence. Often
he says something which is said too seldom, that we shall never
know the truth because evidence is lacking, but equally often the
absence of evidence seems to prove 'the others' wrong. Work on
the Nazi period is complicated by more than average likelihood
that someone said or wrote what they did not mean—for instance,
an anti-Nazi German diplomatist was often obliged to do so. But

SOURCE. Elizabeth Wiskemann in *The Listener*, April 20, 1961. Reprinted
by permission of the author.

arbitrarily to decide that Hitler did not mean what he said, when every probability points to his literal veracity, will hardly do.

The evidence does not count when Mr. Taylor dislikes it. An admirable history recently published in Germany by Professor Bracher and two colleagues quotes from hitherto unrecorded speeches made by Hitler, one, for instance, on February 3, 1933, in which he made quite clear his intention to "conquer new *Lebensraum* in the East and Germanize it ruthlessly." Not only is such evidence brushed aside by Mr. Taylor; he goes further and claims his own insight into Hitler's mind. Hitler, we learn, was saddened by letting the South Tyrolese down, or, in the spring of 1939, when the German press took up the German minority in Poland for the first time since the Polish-German agreement of 1934, Hitler allowed this, "to ease things along as he supposed." How does Mr. Taylor know?

Finally it must be observed that Mr. Taylor's timing is arbitrary too. Chamberlain and Halifax had conversations with Mussolini and Ciano in Rome on January 11, 12, and 13, 1939. "Immediately after the visit," writes Mr. Taylor, "he (Mussolini) told the Germans that he was ready to conclude a formal alliance." In fact Attolico, the Italian Ambassador to Germany, reached Berlin bearing Mussolini's letter to this effect on January 4. The chief mistake made by Chamberlain in Rome may well have been to ask Mussolini about Hitler's possible designs upon the Ukraine. There is reason to suppose that Stalin heard of this question which nourished his suspicions of the West, otherwise so ably described by Mr. Taylor.

Mr. Taylor's admirers will no doubt glory in this new display of "originality of insight and liveliness of style," the criteria of fashion. There are some splendid "cracks" in the book, for instance, about Papen: "He had also been within an ace of being murdered during the purge of June 30, 1934, and was therefore uniquely qualified to persuade the Austrian rulers that Nazi murder attempts should not be taken seriously"—in spite of the murder of Dollfuss. It is nice to know that Mr. Taylor is steadfast in his homage to Dr. Schacht. Otherwise his new book is a virtuoso's display of impish inconsistency in the name of rationality.

<h1>The Economist,
5   Foresight and Hindsight
(Anonymous)</h1>

The searching articles of the Economist *have been compared with the "estimates" the Central Intelligence Agency submits to the White House. However that may be, the anonymous reviews are usually noted for their perception and balanced judgment.*

Mr. Taylor's attempt at a detached analysis of the origins of the German war is already arousing violent controversy; although he himself says that the subject is one nobody bothers with, it has remained very much with us since the end of the war left mankind faced with another, still more colossal, war danger. Statesmen and publicists in Moscow, Bonn, London, Paris and Washington discuss the conduct of east-west relations today in terms of Germany's relations with the powers in the nineteen-thirties. Mr. Taylor is right to the extent that these arguments are not based on any historical study of what happened in 1938 or 1939; more often, the version that is given of those events expresses the statesman's view of what everybody ought (or, more often, ought not) to do now.

Each of the world wars of this century ended with the victors united about the proposition of German war guilt, though unfortunately about little else. German rejection of the charge after the first war took the form of accusing the allies of having really caused the war themselves, by denying Germany the status appropriate to German power, numbers and talents. After the second, dissent has taken a different line—that the allies helped to cause the war by shameful weakness. Kurt Schumacher used to shock westerners (and Russians too, for that matter, though they have often used the argument themselves against the West) by roundly charging the allies with this form of shared responsibility for the disaster. It was largely because this reproach, coming from a German, was found so shocking that Schumacher's party, the German

SOURCE. Anonymous, "Foresight and Hindsight," *Economist*, May 13, 1961. Copyright 1961. Reprinted with permission.

Social Democrats, were labelled as nationalists and therefore un-
reliable, a label they are only now getting free of by turning
nationalist in earnest. Even some leading men of Dr. Adenauer's
party have been heard to chide the British with Munich, a reproach they are curiously reluctant to direct at the French, or
indeed at their own country. British and American writers have
never been lacking to agree with them in assigning a secondary
responsibility for the war to the hesitations and temporising of
the "men of Munich. . . ."

Mr. Taylor, now, looking back, writes a different story, "a story
without heroes and perhaps even without villains." His characters
do what seems, at the time, the obvious thing in defence of the
interests they are concerned with; but, partly because of the
foolish claims they made to higher wisdom and foresight, things
go persistently wrong:

"What was done at Munich mattered less than the way in which
it was done; and what was said about it afterwards counted for
still more."

Mr. Taylor offers no answer to the question whether war might
have been avoided by greater firmness, or by greater conciliation;
merely observing, with a lapse into the wisdom of hindsight, that
"the mixture of the two, practised by the British Government,
was the most likely to fail."

His keenest blow at the accepted view of the origins of the war
is that he questions, as a matter of fact, whether Hitler ever
really had in his mind the definite timetable of aggressive actions
attributed to him by the anti-appeasers at the time, and by nearly
everybody since. After the Munich agreement, in particular, Mr.
Taylor thinks that Hitler had no particular idea what to do next,
and that what he actually did was prompted from outside, by
events.

These controversies are not conducted purely academically, and
their consequences are far from academic. The rejection of German war guilt after 1919 made it easier to demolish the Treaty of
Versailles as a structure, and prepared opinion in the victor countries for retreat in the face of the German re-expansion conducted
by Hitler. After 1945, or at any rate after the Prague coup of
1948, it came to be widely assumed in the West that the Russians
had a set programme of aggressive expansion analogous to Hit-

ler's timetable. The supposed lessons of Munich have been applied as proof that any search for accommodation with the Communist powers would be worse than useless. To dissent from this last proposition, it is not necessary to agree with Mr. Taylor. But equally, one need not agree with all his propositions in order to pay the clarity and penetration of his reconstruction the tribute they deserve.

6   *H. R. Trevor-Roper*
A. J. P. Taylor, Hitler, and the War

H. R. Trevor-Roper is the Regius Professor of Modern History at Oxford University, a post some historians feel should have gone to A. J. P. Taylor. Professor Trevor-Roper has not written any great number of historical works but, as will be seen from the following review article, he is a savagely devastating master of the shorter stroke. His major books include The Last Days of Hitler *(New York, 1947).*

It is over twenty years since the war began. A generation has grown up which never knew the 1930's, never shared its passions and doubts, was never excited by the Spanish civil war, never boiled with indignation against the "appeaser," never lived in suspense from Nuremberg Rally to Nuremberg Rally, awaiting the next hysterical outburst, the next clatter of arms, from the megalomaniac in Berlin. Those of us who knew those days and who try to teach this new generation are constantly made aware of this great gulf between us. How can we communicate across such a gulf the emotional content of those years, the mounting indignation which finally convinced even the "appeasers" themselves that there could be no peace with Hitler, and caused the British people, united in pacifism in 1936, to go, in 1939, united

SOURCE. H. R. Trevor-Roper, "A. J. P. Taylor, Hitler, and the War," *Encounter*, July 1961. Reprinted by permission of A. D. Peters & Company.

into war? For it was not the differing shades of justice in Germany's claims upon the Rhineland, Austria, the Sudetenland, Prague, and Danzig which caused men who had swallowed the first of these annexations to be increasingly evasporated by those which followed and take up arms against the last. It was a changing mood, a growing conviction that all such claims were but pretexts under which Hitler pursued not justice or self-determination for Germany but world-conquest, and that, now or never, he must be stopped. And even across the gulf such a mood must be conveyed by those who teach history to those who learn it: for it is an element in history no less important than the mere facts.

Or is it? Mr. A. J. P. Taylor, it seems, does not think so. He sees the gulf all right, and he wishes to speak to those on the other side of it; but in order to do so, he has decided to lighten the weight he must carry with him. Stripping himself of all personal memories, and thus making himself, in this respect, as naked as they are, he has jumped nimbly across the gulf and now presents himself to them as the first enlightened historian of the future, capable of interpreting the politics of the 1920's and 1930's without any reference to the emotions they engendered, even in himself. Their sole guide, he tells them, must be the documents, which he will select and interpret for them; and indeed, by selection and interpretation, he presents them with a new thesis, illustrated (we need hardly say) with all his old resources of learning, paradox, and *gaminerie*.

The thesis is perfectly clear. According to Mr. Taylor, Hitler was an ordinary German statesman in the tradition of Stresemann and Brüning, differing from them not in methods (he was made Chancellor for "solidly democratic reasons") nor in ideas (he had no ideas) but only in the greater patience and stronger nerves with which he took advantage of the objective situation in Europe. His policy, in so far as he had a policy, was no different from that of his predecessors. He sought neither war nor annexation of territory. He merely sought to restore Germany's "natural" position in Europe, which had been artificially altered by the Treaty of Versailles: a treaty which, for that reason, "lacked moral validity from the start." Such a restoration might involve the recovery of lost German territory like Danzig, but it did not entail the direct government even of Austria or the Sudetenland, let alone Bohemia. Ideally, all that Hitler required was that Austria, Czechoslovakia, and other small Central European states, while remaining independent, should become political satellites of Germany.

Of course it did not work out thus. But that, we are assured, was not Hitler's fault. For Hitler, according to Mr. Taylor, never took the initiative in politics. He "did not make plans—for world-conquest or anything else. He assumed that others would provide opportunities and that he would seize them." And that is what happened. The Austrian crisis of March 1938, we are told, "was provoked by Schuschnigg, not by Hitler." Hitler was positively embarrassed by it: "he was Austrian enough to find the complete disappearance of Austria inconceivable until it happened." Similarly we learn that the Sudeten crisis of 1938 was created by the Sudeten Nazis, who "built up the tension gradually, without guidance from Hitler:" Hitler himself "merely took advantage of it." Having taken advantage of it at Munich, he had no intention of going on and annexing the Czech lands: "he merely doubted whether the settlement would work . . . [he] believed, without sinister intention, that independent Czechoslovakia could not survive when deprived of her natural frontiers and with Czech prestige broken." So, within six months, as "the unforeseen by-product of developments in Slovakia," he felt obliged to tear up the settlement and occupy Prague; but there was "nothing sinister or premeditated" in that. It was an unfortunate necessity forced upon him by the unskillful President Hacha. The Polish crisis of 1939 was similarly forced upon him by Beck. "The destruction of Poland," we are told, "had been no part of his original project. On the contrary, he wished to solve the question of Danzig so that Germany and Poland could remain on good terms." The last thing he wanted was war. The war of nerves was "the only war he understood and liked." Germany "was not equipped to conquer Europe."

"The state of German rearmament in 1939 gives the decisive proof that Hitler was not contemplating general war, and probably not contemplating war at all."

Even on August 23rd, 1939, when the Nazi-Soviet Pact was signed, "both Hitler and Stalin imagined that they had prevented war, not brought it on." What rational person could have supposed that this pact, instead of discouraging the British, would determine them to stand by their commitments? The war, "far from being premeditated, was a mistake, the result on both sides of diplomatic blunders."

Hitler's own share of these diplomatic blunders was, it seems, very small. He "became involved in war," we are told, "through launching on August 29th a diplomatic manoeuvre which he ought to have launched on August 28th." The blunders of the Western statesmen were far more fundamental. For what ought the Western statesmen to have done when faced by Hitler's modest demands? According to Mr. Taylor, they should have conceded them all. They should not have conceded anything to Mussolini, for Mussolini's demands were essentially different from Hitler's. Mussolini was "a vain, blustering boaster" whose government, unlike the "solidly democratic" rule of Hitler, "lived in a state of illegality," and whose demands, since they did not correspond with "reality," were "a fraud." Western statesmen, says Mr. Taylor, lost all claim to respect by recognising such a man. But Hitler was a statesman who merely sought to reassert Germany's "natural weight," and they would therefore have gained respect by recognising him. Accordingly Mr. Taylor's heroes among Western statesmen are those who recognised German claims: Ramsay MacDonald and Neville Chamberlain. Winston Churchill believed in the balance of power and would have maintained frontiers designed on principles of security, not nationality. Intolerable cynicism! How much nobler was that "triumph for British policy," the Munich settlement!

"It was a triumph for all that was best and most enlightened in British life; a triumph for those who had preached equal justice between peoples; a triumph for those who had courageously denounced the harshness and shortsightedness of Versailles."

Munich, according to Mr. Taylor, "atoned" for all the previous weakness of British policy; it was a victory for "morality" (which is his word for political realism); and he praises Chamberlain's "skill and persistence" in bringing "first the French and then the Czechs to follow the moral line." If only Chamberlain had not lost his nerve in 1939! If only he had shown equal "skill and persistence" in enabling Hitler to detach Danzig and the Polish

Corridor, how happy we should all be! Germany would have recovered its "natural" position, "morality" would have triumphed, and everyone would be happy in the best of possible worlds.

Such, in brief, is Mr. Taylor's thesis. It is not surprising that it has been hailed with cries of delight in neo-Nazi or semi-Nazi circles in Germany. It is more surprising that the book has been greeted by the fashionable Grub Street of England as the highest achievement of British historiography. Mr. Taylor has been compared with Gibbon and Macaulay; his failure to secure worthy promotion has caused astonishment. The anonymous oracle of *The Times Literary Supplement* has predicted finality for the result of his "methodical and impeccable logic." In the *Observer*, Mr. Sebastian Haffner (who recently published a panegyric of that "greatest Roman of them all," Dr. Goebbels) has declared the book "an almost faultless masterpiece" in which "fairness reigns supreme;" and his cosy, middlebrow colleagues in rival papers, hypnotised by a reputation which they are unqualified to test, have obediently jollied their readers along in harmony with the blurb. However, let us not all be hypnotised. Before hurling ourselves down the Gadarene slope, let us ask of Mr. Taylor's thesis, not, Is it brilliant? Is it plausible? but, Is it true? By what rules of evidence, by what philosophy of interpretation is it reached?

Perhaps we may begin by noting Mr. Taylor's general philosophy. Mr. Taylor, it seems, does not believe that human agents matter much in history. His story is "a story without heroes, and perhaps even without villains." "In my opinion," he explains, "statesmen are too absorbed by events to follow a preconceived plan. They take one step and the next follows from it." If they achieve anything, it is by accident not design: "all statesmen aim to win: the size of their winnings often surprises them." The real determinants of history, according to Mr. Taylor, are objective situations and human blunders. Objective situations consist of the realities of power; human intelligence is best employed in recognising these realities and allowing events to conform with them; but as human intelligence seldom prevails in politics, the realities generally have to assert themselves, at greater human cost, through the mess caused by human blunders. This doctrine (if I have correctly expressed it) seems remarkably like Mr. E. H. Carr's "realist" doctrine, advanced in his book the *Twenty Years'*

Crisis (1938)—see the *first* edition—a book rightly described by Mr. Taylor as "a brilliant argument in favour of appeasement." Once we accept this general theory, the next stage is easy. All we have to do is to ask ourselves, at what point do we make our calculation of reality? This then provides us with a *datum*. Mr. Taylor takes as his *datum* the spring of 1918. At that time Germany was victorious in the West and triumphant in the East. This, he implies, was the "natural" situation: the Allied victory later in 1918 was artificial—or at least it was made artificial (or, in his words, deprived of "moral validity") by the failure of the Allies to carve Germany up before making peace. This omission left Germany still potentially the greatest power in Europe, naturally tending to revert to the "real" position of January 1918. All that intelligent German statesmen had to do, or indeed could do, was to work hand-in-glove with this "historical necessity"— to their profit. All that Allied statesmen could do was to yield to the same necessity—to their loss. In this sense Hitler and Chamberlain were intelligent statesmen.

But is this general philosophy true? Do statesmen really never make history? Are they, all of them, always "too absorbed by events to follow a preconceived plan"? Was this true of Richelieu, of Bismarck, of Lenin? In particular, was it true of Hitler? Was Hitler really just a more violent Mr. Micawber sitting in Berlin or Berchtesgaden and waiting for something to turn up: something which, thanks to historic necessity, he could then turn to advantage? Certainly Hitler himself did not think so. He regarded himself as a thinker, a practical philosopher, the demiurge of a new age of history. And since he published a blueprint of the policy which he intended to carry out, ought we not at least to look at this blueprint just in case it had some relevance to his policy? After all, the reason why the majority of the British people reluctantly changed, between 1936 and 1939, from the views of Neville Chamberlain and Mr. Taylor to the views of Winston Churchill was their growing conviction that Hitler meant what he said: that he was aiming—*so oder so*, as he used to say—at world conquest. A contemporary conviction that was strong enough to change the mood of a nation from a passionate desire for peace to a resolute determination on war surely deserves some respect from the historian. A historian who totally ignores it because, twenty years later, he can interpret some of the documents in an opposite sense runs the risk of being considered too clever by half.

Let us consider briefly the programme which Hitler laid down for himself. It was a programme of Eastern colonisation, entailing a war of conquest against Russia. If it were successfully carried out, it would leave Germany dominant in Eurasia and able to conquer the West at will. In order to carry it out, Hitler needed a restored German army which, since it must be powerful enough to conquer Russia, must also be powerful to conquer the West if that should be necessary. And that might be necessary even before the attack on Russia. For in order to reach Russia, Hitler would need to send his armies through Poland; and in order to do this —whether by the conquest of Poland or in alliance with it—he would need to break the bond of treaty and interest which bound the new countries of Eastern Europe, the creatures of Versailles, to their creators, Britain and France. Hitler might be able to break those bonds without war against the West, but he could not be sure of it: it was always possible that a war with the West would be necessary before he could march against Russia. And in fact this is what happened.

Now this programme, which Hitler ascribed to himself, and which he actually carried out, is obviously entirely different from the far more limited programme which is ascribed to him by Mr. Taylor, and which he did not carry out. How then does Mr. Taylor deal with the evidence about it? He deals with it quite simply, either by ignoring it or by denying it as inconsistent with his own theories about statesmen in general and Hitler in particular: theories (one must add) for which he produces no evidence at all.

Take the inconvenient fact of Hitler's avowed programme of a great Eastern land-empire. In spite of some casual admission, Mr. Taylor effectively denies that Hitler had any such programme. Hitler, he says, "was always the man of daring improvisations: he made lightning decisions and then presented them as the result of long-term policy." Hitler's *Table Talk*, he says airily (as if this were the only evidence for such a programme), "was delivered far in occupied territory during the campaign against Soviet Russia, and *then* Hitler dreamed of some fantastic empire which would rationalise his career of conquest." [My italics here, and in all quotations below.] But why does Mr. Taylor believe, or rather pretend, that it was only in 1942, after his

Russian conquests, that Hitler dreamed of an Eastern Empire? His programme had been stated, as clearly as possible, in 1924, in *Mein Kampf*, and on numerous other occasions since. Mr. Taylor hardly ever refers to *Mein Kampf* and never to the other occasions. In 1939, he admits, some people "attributed" to Hitler "grandiose plans which *they claimed* to have discovered by reading Mein Kampf in the original (Hitler forbade its publication in English)." The implication is that such plans are not to be found in *Mein Kampf* and that those who "claimed to have discovered" them had not really read, or been able to read, an untranslated work. But the fact is that those plans are unmistakably stated in *Mein Kampf* and that all the evidence of the 1930's showed that Hitler still intended to carry them out. I may add (since Mr. Taylor includes me among those who have ascribed to Hitler "preconceived plans" which he never pursued) that I myself read *Mein Kampf* in the original in 1938, and that I read it under the impact of Munich and of the remarkable prophecies of Sir Robert Ensor, who had read it and who insisted that Hitler meant what he said. By absolutely refusing to face this evidence, and contemptuously dismissing those who have faced it, Mr. Taylor contrives to reach the preposterous conclusion that men like Ensor, who correctly forecast Hitler's future programme from the evidence, were really wrong, and that men like Chamberlain, who did not read the evidence and were proved totally wrong by events, were really right. His sole justification of this paradox is that he has accepted as an axiom a characterisation of Hitler as a "traditional" statesmn pursuing limited aims. Mr. Taylor's Hitler cannot have held such views, and therefore the inconvenient fact that the real Hitler uttered such views with remarkable consistency for twenty years and actually put them into practice, is simply puffed aside. When Hitler, in 1941, finally launched that conquest of Russia which, as he himself said, was "the be-all and end-all of Nazism," Mr. Taylor easily explains it away. "By 1941," he says, "Hitler had lost his old gift of patience:" he "gratuitously" deviated from his former course; and at the mere thought of such an unaccountable fall from grace, Mr. Taylor promptly ends his book.

Nor is this the only perversion of evidence to which Mr. Taylor has to resort, in order to represent Hitler as a "traditional" statesman. The traditional statesman *did not seek*, as Hitler did, to incorporate the Sudeten Germans in the Reich. Traditional statesmen demanded the frontiers of 1914; but Hitler, again and again, repudiated the frontiers of 1914 as a contemptible ambition. They looked back, at most, to the war-aims of 1914; he repudiated those war-aims. Even the "natural" position of January 1918, after the huge gains of Brest-Litovsk gave Germany the Ukraine as a colony of exploitation, a capitalist colony. But Hitler always made it quite clear that he spurned such a colony: he wanted the Ukraine as a colony of settlement. "I should deem it a crime," he said, "if I sacrificed the blood of a quarter of a million men merely for the conquest of natural riches to be exploited in a capitalist way. The goal of the *Ostpolitik* is to open up an area of settlement for a hundred million Germans." All this is pushed aside by Mr. Taylor with the remark,

"when Hitler lamented, 'If only we had a Ukraine . . .' he seemed to suppose there were no Ukrainians. Did he propose to exploit, or exterminate them? *Apparently he never considered the question.*"

As if Hitler had not made his answer perfectly plain! As if he had any scruples about transporting or even exterminating populations! What about the European Jews? But that episode is conveniently forgotten by Mr. Taylor. It does not fit the character of a traditional German statesman who "in principle and doctrine, was no more wicked and unscrupulous than many other contemporary statesmen."

If Mr. Taylor's cardinal assumptions about Hitler's character and purpose are, to say the least, questionable, what are we to say of his use of evidence to illustrate them? Here he states his method with admirable clarity. "It is an elementary part of historical discipline," he says, "to ask of a document not only what is in it but why it came into existence." With this maxim we may agree, only adding that since the contents of a document are objective evidence while its purpose may be a matter of private surmise, we must not rashly subject the former to the latter. Sometimes a man may say the truth even in a document called forth by tactical necessity. At all events, we are not entitled, in defence of an already paradoxical general theory, to assume that he is lying simply because it may not be tactically necessary for him, at that moment, to utter nothing but the truth.

Now let us take a few instances. On November 5th, 1937, Hitler summoned his war-leaders to the Chancellery and made a speech which, he said, in the event of his death was to be regarded as his "last will and testament." That suggests that he was not talking irresponsibly. The official record of this speech is the so-called "Hossbach Memorandum" which was used at Nuremberg as evidence of Hitler's plans for the gradual conquest of Europe. In it Hitler declared that the aim of German policy must be the conquest of *Lebensraum* in Europe, "but we will not copy liberal capitalist policies which rely on exploiting colonies. It is not a case of conquering people but of conquering agriculturally useful space." That seems clear enough. Then Hitler went on to consider the means of making such conquests. "German politics," he said, "must reckon with two hateful enemies, England and France, to whom a strong German colossus in the centre of Europe would be intolerable." Moreover, he admitted, these two hateful enemies would probably, at some stage, resist him by force: "the German question can only be solved by way of force, and this is never without risk." He then proceeded to discuss hypothetical possibilities. Since the hypothetical circumstances did not in fact arise, we need not dwell on them. The essential points are that the risk of European war must be faced by 1943–5, for "after that we can only expect a change for the worse," and that "our first aim" must be, at the first convenient opportunity, "to conquer Czechoslovakia and Austria simultaneously." This first conquest he hoped to achieve without war, for "in all probability England and perhaps also France have already silently written off Czechoslovakia." It could and should therefore be attempted as soon as circumstances make it possible in order that the later, more real risk could be faced before 1943–1945. But there was to be no doubt about the nature of the conquest. It was not to be (as Mr. Taylor always maintains) the reduction of Austria and Czechoslovakia to the role of satellites: it was to be, in Hitler's own words, "the annexation of the two states to Germany, militarily and politically." The idea of satellite states in Eastern Europe, Hitler said in a secret speech delivered only a fortnight later, was one of the futile notions of "traditional" German politicians, and he dismissed it as "idiotic" (*wahnsinnig*). Finally, it is clear that conquered Austria and Czechoslovakia cannot themselves have constituted the *Lebensraum* which was the ultimate objective.

Austria and Czechoslovakia were to be stepping-stones, "in all probability" secured without war, towards larger conquests which would entail a greater risk.

Such was Hitler's "testament" of November 1937. Its content is clear and logical and it has been taken seriously by all historians —until Mr. Taylor comes along and tells us that we have all been hoodwinked. For was not this document produced at Nuremberg? All documents produced at Nuremberg, he says, are "loaded," and "anyone who relies on them finds it almost impossible to escape from the load with which they are charged." So Mr. Taylor gives us a sample of his method of using such documents. Why, he asks, was the speech made? "The historian," he observes, "must push through the *cloud of phrases*" (so much for Hitler's perfectly clear statements) "to the *realities* beneath." The speech, he notes, was not made to Nazis but to generals and admirals, and its purpose was clearly to demand greater rearmament. With this we can agree. But Mr. Taylor does not stop there. In order to persuade these "conservative" war-leaders of the necessity of further rearmament, Hitler (he says) had to overcome the economic opposition of Dr. Schacht. His speech therefore *"had no other purpose"* than "to isolate Schacht from the other conservatives;" the dates 1943–1945 (to which Hitler consistently kept) *"like all such figures, really meant* 'this year, next year, sometime. . . .';" and the content of a speech which Hitler himself described as his political testament (but Mr. Taylor does not quote that description) is dismissed as "day-dreaming unrelated to what followed in real life." Why Hitler should be expected to speak more "realistically" on military matters to Nazis at a froth-blowers' meeting than to hard-headed war-leaders who would have to organise and carry out his programme is not clear. Presumably it is "an elementary part of historical discipline" to assume that.

A second example of Mr. Taylor's "historical discipline" is provided by his treatment of the crisis leading to the outbreak of war in 1939. By now Austria and Czechoslovakia had been "annexed to Germany, militarily and politically," and Hitler had turned the heat upon Poland. According to Mr. Taylor, Hitler really only wanted the German city of Danzig, but since geography prevented him from obtaining it except by the coercion of Poland, he was forced, reluctantly, to apply such coercion and prepare military plans. Of course (according to Mr. Taylor) he did not intend to execute these plans. His military plans were "only intended to reinforce the diplomatic war of nerves." Unfortunately the British Government, misled after Hitler's occupation of Prague into thinking that he aimed at far larger conquests, had imprudently guaranteed Poland and thus threatened Hitler with European war if he sought this next "natural," "moral" aim by any but peaceful means. However, Hitler was a match for this. By making his pact with Russia he effectively countered the British guarantee, and therefore, pushing, like Mr. Taylor, "through the cloud of phrases to the realities beneath," he ignored its empty words and relied, as a rational man, on "the crumbling of Western nerve." Unfortunately, in this case, he miscalculated. Britain, quixotically faithful to the "phrases" of the guarantee, and deluded by the idea that Hitler, if given a free hand, would not stop at Danzig, ignored all the "realities" of the situation and made war, "war for Danzig."

Such is Mr. Taylor's version of the Polish crisis. In defence of it he finds it necessary here, too, to charm away some important documents, and once again it is instructive to watch the exorcist at work. On May 23rd, 1939, Hitler again summoned his war-leaders. He told them, according to Mr. Taylor, who quotes no other words of the document, "there will be war. Our task is to isolate Poland. . . . It must not come to a simultaneous showdown with the West." "This," comments Mr. Taylor, "seems clear enough;" but he then dismisses even this evidence by saying authoritatively that "when Hitler talked to his generals, he talked for effect, not to reveal the workings of his mind." So that is that. Three months later, with the signature of the Nazi-Soviet Pact, Hitler again addressed his generals, and again Mr. Taylor is content to quote only one sentence from the speech: "now the probability is great that the West will not intervene." Apart from that "hard core," the rest of the speech, he says, can be ignored, as Hitler "was talking for effect." After all, by the Nazi-Soviet Pact, Hitler considered that "he had prevented war, not brought it on." So, once again, Hitler's mere "phrases" dissolve on contact with Mr. Taylor's "realities."

But why should we suppose, as an axiom, that Hitler, when briefing his generals on the eve of a possible war, talked only for effect? Why should we not suppose that he intended them to be ready (as they were) for the real future? And why should we altogether overlook some very clear statements which he made to them? For if we look at the full texts of these two speeches, we find that Mr. Taylor has made certain remarkable omissions.

In the first of these two speeches Hitler began by insisting that the next step towards Germany's goal could not be taken "without the invasion of foreign states or attacks upon foreign property," and that although bloodless victories had been won in the past, "further successes cannot be obtained without the shedding of blood." "*Danzig*," he went on, in words from which Mr. Taylor has firmly averted his eyes, "*is not the subject of the dispute at all. It is a question of expanding our living-space in the East.*" Moreover, he looked clearly forward to the prospect of war with the West. "The Polish problem," he said, "is inseparable from conflict with the West." For all that, "we are left with the decision to attack Poland at the first opportunity. We cannot expect a repetition of the Czech affair." Of course Hitler hoped to avoid a simultaneous conflict with the West, but he did not rely on any such hope: "the Führer doubts the possibility of a peaceful settlement with England. We must prepare ourselves for the conflict." The remaining two-thirds of the document deal with the problems of war with Britain, "the driving-force against Germany." All this is totally ignored by Mr. Taylor: it cannot have been the "hard core" of any argument used by *his* Hitler: therefore, he declares, it was mere froth, uttered for "effect."

In the second speech Hitler similarly made clear statements which Mr. Taylor does not quote. For instance, immediately after the "hard core," the single sentence which he does quote, about the probability that the West will be frightened out of intervention by the Nazi-Soviet Pact, come the words, "*we must accept the risk with reckless resolution*"; and Hitler then went on to explain how Germany, thanks to Russian supplies, could withstand a Western blockade. His only fear, he said, was that "at the last moment some *Schweinhund* will make a proposal for mediation:" a proposal, perhaps, which might have fobbed him off with Danzig which, as he had admitted, was "not the subject of the dispute at all." No: Hitler was now resolved on war, even if the West did come in.

"I shall give a propagandist cause for starting the war: never mind if it be plausible or not. The victor shall not be asked afterwards whether he told the truth or not."

As for the West, "even if war should break out in the West, the destruction of Poland shall be the primary objective." Which indeed was exactly what happened. By last-minute diplomatic manoeuvres Hitler naturally sought to detach the West, but when that could not be done, he went ahead, with his eyes open, into a European war which, though larger than he had hoped, he still reckoned on winning.

I have said enough to show why I think Mr. Taylor's book utterly erroneous. In spite of his statements about "historical discipline," he selects, suppresses, and arranges evidence on no principle other than the needs of his thesis; and that thesis, that Hitler was a traditional statesman, of limited aims, merely responding to a given situation, rests on no evidence at all, ignores essential evidence, and is, in my opinion, demonstrably false. This casuistical defence of Hitler's foreign policy will not only do harm by supporting neo-Nazi mythology: it will also do harm, perhaps irreparable harm, to Mr. Taylor's reputation as a serious historian.

But why, we may ask, has he written it? Is it, as some have suggested, a gesture of posthumous defiance to his former master, Sir Lewis Namier, in revenge for some imagined slight? If so, it is just as well that it is posthumous: otherwise what devastating justice it would have received! There would have been no nonsense then about "impeccable logic" in *The Times Literary Supplement*! Or is it, as Mr. Taylor's friends prefer to believe, mere characteristic *gaminerie*, the love of firing squibs and laying banana-skins to disconcert the gravity and upset the balance of the orthodox? Or does Mr. Taylor perhaps suppose that such a reinterpretation of the past will enable us better to face the problems of the present? Theoretically this should not be his motive, for not only does Mr. Taylor, in this book, frequently tell us that the past has never pointed the course of the future, but he has also assured us recently, in the *Sunday Express*, that the study of history can teach nothing, not even general understanding: its sole purpose, he says, is to amuse; and it would therefore seem to have no more right to a place in education than the blowing of soap-bubbles or other forms of innocent recreation. It may therefore be that Mr. Taylor merely means to amuse, not to instruct, by his irresponsible antics. Nevertheless, Mr. Taylor is not noted for consistency and it may be that, in this instance, he does see a connection between the past and the present, a lesson for our times. At any rate, it may be worth while to point out lessons which might logically be deduced from Mr. Taylor's version of history, if it were accepted as uncritically by the public as it has been by their guides, the weekly reviewers.

Basically, the problem is that of the outbreak of world wars, according to Mr. Taylor, the second World War had a double origin: first, it was "implicit" in the general situation; secondly, it was made explicit by the particular blunders of statesmen in the face of that situation. The general situation was created in 1918 when the victorious Allies did not carve Germany up, and so made the ultimate recovery of its "natural weight" inevitable. The particular blunders lay in the failure of Western statesmen to draw the logical conclusions and yield to the inevitable. If only they had shown "realism" and yielded to all Hitler's demands, they would have found them limited and reasonable: it was only war and victory which surprised him by the size of his winnings and made him think of world-conquest.

Now let us transfer these doctrines from the 1930's to the 1950's. The inference is clear. First, the victorious Allies in 1945 did (however unintentionally) carve Germany up, and so (if they will only keep it divided) their settlement of the German problem is "morally valid," and new German aggression is to be feared. Secondly, in the new circumstances thus created, "realism" consists in allowing the new great power which has replaced Germany in Europe to assert its "natural weight." Mr. Khrushchev, we should recognise, has no more ambitions of world-conquest than Hitler. He is a traditional Russian statesman of limited aims, and "the moral line" consists in letting him have his way more completely than we let Hitler have his: in other words, unilateral disarmament. Perhaps in this one respect Mr. Taylor does display "methodical and impeccable logic."

[Mr. Taylor retorted in *Encounter*, September 1961.]

"HOW TO QUOTE: EXERCISES FOR BEGINNERS"

Trevor-Roper (*Encounter*, July 1961)	*Taylor* (*Origins of the Second World War*)
According to Mr. Taylor . . . Hitler merely sought to restore	Hitler, too, wanted to free Germany from the restrictions of the

Germany's "natural" position in Europe, which had been artificially altered by the Treaty of Versailles.

peace treaty; to restore a great German army; and then to make Germany the greatest power in Europe from her natural weight. . . . Maybe his ambitions were genuinely limited to the East; maybe conquest there would have only been the preliminary to conquest in Western Europe or on a world scale. No one can tell.

For what ought the Western statesmen to have done when faced by Hitler's modest demands? According to Mr. Taylor, they should have conceded them all.

Wiser counsels were not lacking. Early in July [1939] Count von Schwerin, of the German War Ministry, was in England. He spoke frankly: "Hitler took no account of words, only of deeds. . . ." This advice was disregarded. . . . The British statesmen were trying to strike a balance between firmness and conciliation; and, being what they were, inevitably struck the wrong one.

Winston Churchill believed in the balance of power and would have maintained frontiers designed on principles of security, not nationality. Intolerable cynicism!

It [Churchill's] was a view which shocked most Englishmen and which, by its apparent cynicism, deprived its holders of influence on policy.

Munich, according to Mr. Taylor, "atoned" for all the previous weaknesses of British policy. He [Taylor] praises Chamberlain's "skill and persistence" in bringing "first the French and then the Czechs to follow the moral line."

Idealists could claim that British policy had been tardy and hesitant. In 1938 it atoned for these failings. With skill and persistence, Chamberlain brought first the French, and then the Czechs, to follow the moral line.

If only Chamberlain had not lost his nerve in 1939! If only he had shown equal "skill and persistence" in enabling Hitler to detach Danzig and the Polish Corridor, how happy we should all be!

Men will long debate whether this renewed war [of 1939] could have been averted by greater firmness or by greater conciliation; and no answer will be found to these hypothetical speculations. Maybe either would have succeeded, if consistently followed; the mixture of the two, practised by the British Government, was the most likely to fail.

The reason why the majority of the British people changed, between 1936 and 1939, from the views of Neville Chamberlain and Mr. Taylor to the views of Winston Churchill was their growing conviction that was strong enough to change the mood of a nation . . . surely deserves some respect from the historian. A historian who ignores it . . . runs the risk of being considered too clever by half.

There followed an underground explosion of public opinion such as the historian cannot trace in precise terms. . . . All the prophets had said that Hitler would never rest content; he would march from one conquest to another, and could be stopped only by force or the threat of force. Like water dropping on a stone, their voices suddenly broke through the crust of incredulity. They seemed to have been proved right; and the "appeasers" wrong. . . . Henceforth the appeasers were on the defensive, easily distracted from their work and hardly surprised at their own failure.

But what about the European Jews? That episode is conveniently forgotten by Mr. Taylor.

Many Germans had qualms as one act of persecution followed another culminating in the unspeakable wickedness of the gas-chambers. But few knew how to protest. Everything which Hitler did against the Jews followed logically from the racial doctrines in which most Germans vaguely believed.

It does not fit the character of a German statesman who "in principle and doctrine, was no more wicked and unscrupulous than many other statesmen."

In principle and doctrine Hitler was no more wicked and unscrupulous than many other contemporary statesmen. In wicked acts he outdid them all.

According to Mr. Taylor, Hitler really only wanted the German city of Danzig, but since geography prevented him from obtain-

Previously Danzig might have been settled without implying any upheaval in international relations. Now it had become the symbol

ing it except by the coercion of Poland, he was forced, reluctantly, to apply such coercion and prepare military plans. Of course (according to Mr. Taylor) he did not intend to execute these plans.

of Polish independence; and, with the Anglo-Polish alliance, of British independence as well. Hitler no longer wished merely to fulfill German national aspirations or to satisfy the inhabitants of Danzig. He aimed to show that he had imposed his will on the British and on the Poles. They, on their side, had to deny him this demonstration. . . . Of course Hitler's nature and habits played their part. It was easy for him to threaten, and hard for him to conciliate.

It [the book] will do harm, perhaps irreparable harm, to Mr. Taylor's reputation as a serious historian.

The Regius Professor's methods of quotation might also do harm to his reputation as a serious historian, if he had one.

[In the same issue of *Encounter*, Professor Trevor-Roper gave "A Reply."]

I am afraid that after examining Mr. Taylor's use of German documents, I am not disposed to accept him as a tutor in the art of quotation. Nor do I think that his "exercises" amount to much. They are calculated to spare him the trouble of argument and to give a lot of trouble to the reader. They are certainly no answer to the positive points made in my review.

In my review I tried to summarise Mr. Taylor's thesis. Of course such a summary is not tied exclusively to single quotations: it is distilled from many; and it is not refuted by single quotations which in no case conflict seriously with it but, at most, may sometimes illustrate only a part of it or vary the emphasis. In view of the bewildering inconsistencies in Mr. Taylor's own presentation of his thesis (some, but only some, of which have been shown by correspondence in *The Times Literary Supplement*), such variations are not hard to find.

For instance, my sentence No. 1 is not based only on the passage which Mr. Taylor now places opposite it. It is also based on other passages in his book. Thus . . . he writes, "Hitler wanted the

Allies to accept the verdict of January 1918; to abandon the artificial undoing of this verdict after November 1918, and to acknowledge that Germany had been victorious in the East. This was not a preposterous programme;" and . . . "whatever his long-term plans (and it is doubtful whether he had any) the mainspring of his immediate policy had been 'the destruction of Versailles.' " I cannot see that my summary is unfair.

Similarly, in quotation 9, if Mr. Taylor's own words are boiled down, what do they come to? In this single quotation he is saying that in the material world Hitler only wanted Danzig, but that, by now, he wanted to get it by means which would constitute a prestige victory . . . he explains that, for geographical reasons, Danzig could not be seized without direct coercion of Poland. In other passages, quoted by me, Mr. Taylor insists that Hitler did not want war but only a war of nerves backed by military force. My words, which quotation 9 is intended to refute, seem a fair summary of these passages. And the same can be said, I believe, of all the other "exercises."

In one "exercise" (No. 6) Mr. Taylor suggests that I have overlooked a paragraph in his book. I have not. I said that "a contemporary conviction that was strong enough to change the mood of a nation . . . surely deserves some respect from the historian," "Respect," not "notice." By "respect" I mean that the historian should consider whether such a "conviction" may have been based on sound reasons. I do not mean that he should merely note the change in mood, dismiss the arguments, and pass on.

I could make the same point about "exercise" No. 7. When I wrote that Mr. Taylor conveniently forgot the persecution of the Jews, I meant, of course, that he drew no deductions from a fact central to the evaluation of Hitler's rule and methods and particularly relevant to the question of the disposal of "inferior" races. I do not regard this serious problem as faced, or my statement as exploded, by a single parenthetical reference in which a crime unique in European history is flicked aside as the logical result of generally shared German ideas.

In "exercise" No. 8 Mr. Taylor suggests that I have deliberately omitted a distinction which he made between Hitler's relatively innocent principles and doctrines and his admittedly wicked acts. But I scrupulously quoted his limiting words "in principle and doctrine." And anyway, if his wicked acts are to be dismissed as merely "following logically" from his innocent "doctrines," what is the force of the distinction?

If Mr. Taylor had been able to convict me of any "quotation" comparable with his own version of the German documents (a subject on which he is now silent), or if he had shown my summary to be inconsistent with his thesis as he so often is with himself (an inconsistency on which—see his letter to *The Times Literary Supplement*—he has also refused to comment), I should indeed be ashamed. But if these "exercises" represent the sum of his answer to my criticism, I am unmoved.

7   *Ian F. D. Morrow*
         in International Affairs

This review in the leading English journal of contemporary world problems, International Affairs, *focuses on a point missed by many critics: "the standpoint from which Mr. Taylor writes."*

Always an *enfant terrible* among historians, Mr. Taylor has now unconcernedly let loose a hawk amid the academic dovecotes to tear preconceived and traditional notions to pieces and inevitably to provoke noisy flutterings and shrill cries of outraged and alarmed protest. Critics of this highly controversial and challenging yet withal stimulating and very readable account of the origins of the second World War have accused Mr. Taylor of committing nearly all the sins comprised in the historian's decalogue. Glaringly contradictory statements have rightly been discovered in these pages; moral considerations are said to have been ignored or minimized; the protagonists in the bloodiest drama of history have been set on a level of nebulous grayness

SOURCE. Ian F. D. Morrow in *International Affairs*, October 1961. Reprinted by permission of the author.

where blame for what happened seems to rest almost equally and indifferently upon all their shoulders. It has also been justly said that Mr. Taylor often neglects to furnish substantiating evidence for the many—there are indeed a great many—startlingly controversial statements which he makes and which have the delusive appearance of being delivered *ex cathedra,* although in fact they are only expressions of personal opinion. Many of these criticisms are undoubtedly justifiable. Yet when all have been taken into account it seems to the present reviewer that Mr. Taylor's learned critics have failed to comprehend or else have ignored the standpoint from which Mr. Taylor writes. It is certainly *not* an accepted traditional academic standpoint. On the contrary, Mr. Taylor expressly states as early as . . . that he has "attempted to tell the story *as it may appear to some future historian* (my italics), working from the records."

Mr. Taylor with disturbing originality has discovered or perhaps invented a new form of history—*imaginable* history. The judgments and opinions liberally scattered over these pages are not necessarily Mr. Taylor's own *real* opinions and judgments. They are simply the opinions and judgments which Mr. Taylor rightly or wrongly imagines will be held and formed by an as yet unborn historian writing in fifty or one hundred years' time. As an experiment in this new form of history Mr. Taylor's coruscating volume is nothing less than a *tour de force.* Clio owes him a measure of gratitude for some light relief from her habitual serious reading.

8   *David Marquand*
              in The New Statesman

This review in The New Statesman, *a political and literary
periodical to which Mr. Taylor himself often contributes book
reviews, is representative of the mixed response of the English
press to the* Origins.

Mr. A. J. P. Taylor is the only English historian now writing
who can bend the bow of Gibbon and Macaulay. Like them,
and in spite of his own coy assertions to the contrary he writes to
prove a doctrine. Reduced to its simplest form, the Taylor Doctrine states that everything happens by chance. Statesmen do not
plan ahead; and if they do, their plans do not come true. If,
as frequently happens, they claim after the event that their most
successful *coups* were planned in advance, that merely shows that
statesmen are incorrigible liars. If, as happens more rarely, what
appears to have been a premeditated plan appears to have succeeded, that merely shows that appearances are often deceptive—
or that even statesmen are sometimes lucky. The great statesman
scorns forethought: it is the mark of genius to leap before you
look. For history is not a tram, as the young man in the limerick
supposed. It is not even a bus. If anything, it is a road accident.

Armed with this doctrine, Taylor has already demolished one of
the most plausible myths of modern history: the conventional
theory that German unification was the fruit of Bismarck's uncanny skill as a long-range planner. Bismarck emerges from his
biography, not as the patient architect of the Second Reich, but
as an improviser of genius whose greatest triumphs were unforeseen, and perhaps even unsought. Now Taylor has turned his
doctrine onto a later and still more painful phase of Germany's
painful relations with her neighbours. The result is a master-

SOURCE. David Marquand, "The Taylor Doctrine," *New Statesman,* April
21, 1961. Reprinted from the *New Statesman,* London, by permission.

piece: lucid, compassionate, beautifully written in a bare, sparse style, and at the same time deeply disturbing. It is disturbing in the way that all good history is disturbing (and all good art for that matter). Sir Lewis Namier once suggested that history should be for society what psychoanalysis is for the individual. Societies, like individuals, could become obsessively and self-destructively fixated on past experiences. The historian's proper function was to enable his readers to overcome the past, by understanding it. Namier's analogy is not altogether satisfactory, and can easily be pushed too far. But it seems to me profoundly relevant to contemporary Britain, and to Taylor's book. For Britain today shows all the signs of neurotic fixation on a number of episodes in her past: on the supposed, and largely fictitious, glories of her peaceful evolution to responsible government; on the even more obviously fictitious glories of Empire miraculously transformed into Commonwealth; and—most dangerous of all—on the quite genuine glories of her solitary stand in 1940, and the quite false implications which have been drawn from it.

1940, to most Englishmen who remember it, was the last "annus mirabilis" in English history: the year when Britain, the innocent victim of continental wickedness and domestic blindness, betrayed by the Russians and let down by the French, stood alone against the world—and triumphed. The moral of the conventional story is that continentals are not to be trusted; that Britain's destiny is quite separate from Europe's and that in the last resort Europe does not matter anyway. Like all such myths, this rests on the assumption that the British people were innocent victims of other people's wickedness—for if they were no more innocent than their neighbours, their escape in 1940 ceases to be a proof of moral superiority, and becomes a piece of unmerited good luck. Such a conclusion would be intolerable; and so the myth-makers have been at work. In the Right-wing version, the guilty men were all continental Europeans (though abetted by the folly of the British Left). Britain, not realising that Hitler was plotting to enslave the world, tried patiently to meet his reasonable demands. When his demands grew unreasonable, she took up arms to save the liberties of Europe—undeterred by the knowledge that the conspirators of Berlin had by then made a deal with the equally sinister conspirators of Moscow. In the Left-wing version, the guilty men were to be found in Whitehall as well as in the Wilhelmstrasse—but the British people had no share in the guilt of their rulers. Baldwin and Chamberlain, at heart sympathetic to fascism, wilfully deceived the British people, ignored the warnings of the Opposition and the lesson of the facts, and encouraged the dictators on their career of world conquest by failing to stand up to them until it was too late.

Taylor has exploded these myths, by exploding the assumptions of guilt and innocence on which they rest. In his version, no one is guilty, which is another way of saying that no one is innocent. No one planned the Second World War: not Hitler, and certainly not Chamberlain, Mussolini or Stalin. Hitler's domestic policy was undoubtedly vicious and evil. But his foreign policy was no worse (though no better, of course) than that of any other self-respecting German Government: to undo the Versailles settlement, and to make Germany once again the dominant power on the European continent. Taylor's Hitler, like his Bismarck, was not a conspirator at all. He was a feckless improviser, whose real genius lay in seizing unexpected opportunities when they were presented to him. His loudly proclaimed plans for world conquest were dreams, not blue-prints. His greatest successes were the accidental results of other men's expedients. The Anschluss was provoked by Schuschnigg, not by Hitler. The settlement at Munich was "a triumph for British policy . . . not a triumph for Hitler, who started with no such clear intention." The German establishment of a protectorate over Bohemia in March 1939 was "the unforeseen by-product of developments in Slovakia." The war came when it did because Hitler rightly suspected that the British secretly wanted him to take Danzig, and launched "on 29 August a diplomatic manoeuvre which he ought to have launched on 28 August."

But if Hitler did not "cause" the war, who did? Stalin—the alternative scapegoat of the Right? Or Chamberlain—the alternative preferred by the Left? Taylor dismisses both answers. Stalin, as he is depicted here, was as much the victim of his own and other people's mistakes as the Western leaders were. The Nazi-Soviet pact, so far from being conclusive proof of Soviet wickedness, was the Russians' only way out of an impossible situation. As Communists, they were in any case prone to suspect that Britain and France might welcome a German drive to the East—a suspicion which Britain (though not France) did nothing to remove. During the Czech crisis, the Russians at least said that they would honour their commitments, and they may even have meant it. The British sold out, not the Russians; and if Britain would not fight for Czechoslovakia, it was reasonable to suppose that she would not fight for the Soviet Union either. In Taylor's view, this supposition was probably justified. Britain wanted an alliance with Russia, insofar as she wanted one at all, as a moral demonstration not as a commitment to action. What the British wanted was that "Russian assistance should be turned on and off at will, like a tap; and that they, or maybe the Poles, should alone be entitled to turn it." It is hardly surprising that Stalin should have preferred to turn his own tap, even at the price of a pact with Hitler. . . .

Taylor's picture of Hitler in itself goes some way towards excusing Baldwin and Chamberlain. After all, the British Government could hardly be blamed for not knowing what Hitler's plans were if he did not know them himself. It is true, of course, that there was an insane streak in Hitler to which Taylor does not do justice. But the chances that a madman will come to power in any country, let alone in a civilised country in the heart of Europe, are so small that it may be wiser to assume that your opponents are sane, until you have conclusive proof of the contrary. During the war, no doubt, Hitler did give conclusive proof of insanity; but Chamberlain can hardly be blamed for not knowing in 1938 what Hitler would have become by 1942.

In any case, even supposing that Baldwin and Chamberlain could have inferred Hitler's latest wickedness from the evidence of his internal policy, what follows? Is one justified in going to war because one dislikes another country's internal arrangements? Perhaps: but not according to the prevailing Left-wing theory of the time. The Left had steadily denounced, and still denounces, the allied intervention in Russia after the First World War. But if it was wrong to intervene against Soviet tyranny, why would it have been right to intervene against the Nazis? In any case, when would the intervention have taken place: before Hitler had become dangerous, or afterwards? Intervention in Germany before she had become a menace would have been a flagrant act of preventive war, and would have been denounced by all right-thinking people, and perhaps repudiated by the British people. Intervention after Hitler had built up his forces meant risking a European war, which no one wanted—least of all the Labour Party. . . .

If Taylor's book has a lesson, it is just that there were no crimes, only mistakes; that Europe died at her own hand, not at the hand of any one man or nation; and that to search for scapegoats is to sin against the historian's Holy Ghost.

9   *F. H. Hinsley*
The Origins of the Second World War

F. H. Hinsley, a Cambridge University scholar of diplomatic history, is an expert on the causes of war, with which he deals in his major work, Power and the Pursuit of Peace *(Cambridge, 1963).*

Mr. A. J. P. Taylor is not a didactic writer. In his latest book the key to the structure of his thinking on the subject is tucked away about a third of the way through. "Wars," he writes there, "are much like road accidents. They have a general cause and particular causes at the same time. Every road accident is caused in the last resort by the invention of the internal combustion engine and by men's desires to get from one place to another. . . . But . . . the police and the courts do not weigh profound causes. They seek a specific cause for each accident—error on the part of the driver, excessive speed, drunkenness, faulty brakes, bad road surface. So it is with wars. 'International anarchy' makes war possible; it does not make it certain. . . . Both enquiries make sense on different levels. They are complementary, they do

SOURCE. F. H. Hinsley, "The Origins of the Second World War," *Historical Journal,* 1961. Reprinted by permission of Cambridge University Press.

not exclude each other. The Second World War, too, had profound causes, but it also grew out of specific events, and these events are worth detailed examination."

This is a good point of departure, though we shall later suggest some qualifications and improvements to it. Confusion and disagreement about the causes of wars have arisen essentially from the failure to make this distinction between the given conditions that make war possible, or even quite likely to occur, and the events and the decisions that immediately lead to it.

When we turn to Mr. Taylor's application of this insight to the causes of war in 1939—not so good. He is content to dismiss as "profound causes" for the Second World War factors to which serious scholars have never given any credence and, this done, he almost urges that it has no profound causes at all. His interpretation of the specific events which led to the war is distorted by equally serious errors in logic. To make matters worse, the whole book is written in the commendable cause of historical objectivity—he has "attempted to tell the story as it may appear to some future historian, working from records; the result may be to demonstrate how much historians miss or misunderstand" —but is an outstanding example of how even a scholar is not immune from the temptation to pour out the baby with the bathwater.

As the first quotation suggests, he is more interested, personally, in the specific events that led to the Second World War than in whatever may have been its profound causes. We cannot object on this score; "both enquiries make sense on different levels." But nobody who has both levels in mind can write a book on the origins of the Second World War without giving some attention to the profound causes. Mr. Taylor duly, though somewhat perfunctorily, deals with them—or, rather, he deals with those "profound causes" of the war that occupied the attention of the public at the time, and he discusses them only to dismiss them— quite rightly—as rubbish.

In the 1930's the League collapsed and Europe returned to the "international anarchy." "Many people, including some historians, believe that this in itself is enough to explain the Second World War. And so, in a sense, it is. So long as states admit no restriction of their sovereignty, wars will occur between them. . . .

The defect of this explanation is that, since it explains everything, it explains nothing. If "international anarchy" invariably caused war, then the states of Europe should never have known peace since the close of the middle ages." "Men also said that Fascism 'inevitably' produced war." In fact, although Hitler and Mussolini did glorify war and use the threat of it to promote their aims, statesmen had done this throughout history and "that there had been long periods of peace . . . despite the fiery talk." In any case "the Fascist dictators would not have gone to war unless they had seen a chance of winning, and the cause of war was therefore as much the blunders of others as the wickedness of the dictators themselves." Another argument has been that capitalism inevitably led to the war; but "here was another general explanation which explained everything and nothing. . . . The great capitalist states . . . were the most anxious to avoid war; and in every country, including Germany, capitalists were the class most opposed to war. Indeed, if one were to indict the capitalists of 1939, it would be for pacifism and for timidity . . . ." As for the special version of this case which argues that the Fascist states represented the last aggressive stage of capitalism in decline—that their economic momentum could be sustained only by war—their economics did not rely on armaments and they were militarily unready when war broke out.

There is nothing wrong—or not much—with these statements. (There is nothing new about them either: historians, as opposed to the public, have dismissed these fallacies long ago; perhaps even the public has discarded them by now.) When, however, Mr. Taylor has thus pushed "through the cloud of phrases to the realities beneath," which is what, as he rightly says, the historian must try to do, he takes up the position that, since these so-called "profound causes" of the war are so much rubbish, the war had no profound causes at all. The remaining two-thirds of this book are occupied with the details of the international crises that took place between 1936 and 1939. There is hardly another word about anything except the specific incidents that led to the War. If the War had profound causes, as he has told us it did, we never learn what they were.

Earlier on, it is true, we have learned something which is relevant to the problem and which, if we are familiar with the subject, we can apply to the emergency. The earlier pages of the book contain some wise words. By the armistice of 1918 the Germans recognized defeat; "in return—and almost without realizing it—the Allies acknowledged the German Government." Similarly the Treaty of Versailles was a valuable German asset—it was designed to provide security against German aggression but could only work with the cooperation of the German Government. "The most important thing in the treaty was that it was concluded with a united Germany." This again was done "without deliberation." Since she was left intact Germany was bound to resist the Versailles Treaty from the outset, and she "fought specifically in the Second World War to reverse the verdict of the first and to destroy the settlement which followed it." Since the Allies had decided to leave Germany intact their policy necessarily assumed that "sooner or later she must return to the comity of nations," and "so far as there was a coherent pattern in the postwar years it was the story of efforts to conciliate Germany and of their failure."

Mr. Taylor makes equally clear the reasons for this failure. Germany was not only left intact; she was left immensely strong relatively. She remained in existence; Europe's other Empires, the Ottoman, the Austrian and the Russian, had all collapsed. (He might have added that France had been gravely weakened.) She had only to shake off the restrictions imposed by the Treaty of Versailles to emerge "as strong, or almost as strong, as she had been in 1914." (It would be nearer the mark to say, as later he does say, that she emerged relatively much stronger than in 1914.) The allies were led by their own policy to treating Germany as an equal, but if she were treated as an equal she would be the strongest power. "The German problem was not German aggressiveness or militarism, or the wickedness of her rulers. These . . . merely aggravated the problem. . . . The essential problem was political not moral. However democratic or pacific Germany might become, she remained by far the greatest Power on the continent of Europe; with the disappearance of Russia, more so than before." (What a refreshing change this is from his earlier views.) Her recovery from Versailles was accordingly "unprecedented in its speed and strength." The upshot was that, whereas "before 1914 there had been a Balance," "the constellation of

Europe was [now] profoundly changed—and to Germany's advantage." "The old balance of power which formerly did something to restrain Germany, had broken down." "If events followed their course in the old free' way, nothing could prevent the Germans from overshadowing Europe, even if they did not plan to do so."

There is little to quarrel with in these conclusions, either. The emphasis on Allied absence of mind and lack of deliberation in making the armistice and the Treaty is misleading. It implies that it was a practicable possibility to occupy and partition Germany in 1918, which is not the case, and that if Germany had then been occupied and partitioned there would not have been another European war, which is questionable. Mr. Taylor has, however, previously gone some way towards recognizing this by saying that the decision to grant the German government an armistice was taken "from the highest and most sensible motives." The argument that the Treaty was an asset to Germany in that it presupposed German cooperation sounds less impressive when it is remembered that all treaties have this drawback. Otherwise with one notable exception, the conclusions fairly represent the best current opinion among historians about the profound causes of the Second World War, about the given conditions that made it quite likely that a war would break out.

This opinion does not hold that the international anarchy—in the sense of the existence of separate sovereign states—invariably produces war, but it knows that conditions of acute international unbalance invariably tend to invite it. It does not believe that Fascism and capitalism, inevitably led to war, if only because it has studied the restraint of political societies, both Fascist and non-Fascist, in conditions of balance and the absence of restraint that even democratic societies can display in the opposite conditions. But it knows that Fascism was exacerbated by the acute international unbalance of the inter-war years —that if the Fascist dictators would not have gone to war unless they had seen a chance of winning, it was this which offered them the chance of winning—just as it knows that the blunders of the Western Powers were due not only to their ineptitude and timidity but also to the enormous dimensions of the problem which the international unbalance presented to them. There was ineptitude; Mr. Taylor is right to say that these powers, and also the United States and Russia, were too slow to realize the need to restore the balance to contain Germany; but if they were too slow it was because Germany's return to predominance was so fast.

It knows indeed—and this is the notable exception to the validity of these conclusions—that precisely because the unbalance was so extreme it is wrong to state that Germany fought the Second World War "specifically . . . to reverse the verdict of the first and to destroy the settlement which followed it." It would prefer to support the other statements he makes, in contradiction of this one and to the effect that she fought for something more: that Hitler's and Mussolini's appetite for success was "greater" than is normal, that "nothing could prevent the Germans from overshadowing Europe, even if they did not plan to do so." It even knows that the unbalance was such that they could not avoid planning to do so. To return to Mr. Taylor's analogy, it would say that every road accident is caused in the last resort not so much by the invention of the internal combustion engine and by men's desire to get from one place to another as by the absence of restraints and conditions that make for careful driving; that every war is caused in the last resort not so much by the "international anarchy" as by the absence of similar restraints and conditions within the international system.

If we cannot disagree with the main drift of these conclusions neither can we grumble that Mr. Taylor does not mention their relevance to the profound causes of the war. On this point, too, the early pages contain good sense. Whatever Germany fought for, "the first war explains the second and, in fact, caused it, in so far as one event causes another." With regard to her success in remaining united and strong, "the Second World War grew out of the victories in the first and out of the way in which these victories were used." The decision to leave her strong and united "ultimately led to the Second World War." It is in spite of these early remarks that he makes no reference to any profound cause of the war after he has reached the year 1936. And it is largely because he later forgets this evidence for the acute unbalance resulting from the first war, and loses all interest in its bearing on the outbreak of the second, that he can arrive at such an extraor-

dinary version of those "specific events" which took place when
the unbalance had come into the open.

Before demonstrating how this is so it is necessary to uncover
two other errors in logic which are closely related and which
enter directly into his treatment of those events. Just as his interpretation of the crises that began in 1938 is central to the doubt
he casts, at the beginning of the book, on the view that Hitler
"planned the Second World War," that "his will alone caused it,"
so it is central to his analysis of these crises that in no case was
German policy the cause of them. All that his evidence can be
strained to yield, on the most generous of conditions, is that German planning did not actually occasion these crises. He never sees
the difference between general policy and precise planning or between cause and occasion. The police and the courts, though they
confine themselves to specific events, surely try to avoid these elementary errors.

He does not deny that Germany had a policy. In the sense of
his having had a precise schedule, it is not the accepted view,
as Mr. Taylor says it is, that Hitler was "deliberately preparing
from the first a great war which would . . . make him master of
the world." The authorities who hold some such view base themselves on Hitler's developing aims, not on his possession from
the start of plans for precise action at precise dates. Who would
be so naive? Essentially, moreover, Mr. Taylor does not disagree
with these authorities as much as he frequently professes to do.
Does he himself think Hitler had any aims? He had "day-dreams,"
as revealed in *Mein Kampf* and on many later occasions, but
these did not affect his policy. But did he have any policy? Well,
yes, he did. There was nothing "original" about it, but it was
his policy to free Germany from the peace treaty, to give her
once more a great army and to make her the greatest power in
Europe "from her natural weight." "Fundamentally he was not
interested merely in revising Germany's frontiers. He wanted to
make Germany dominant in Europe . . . ." To the extent that
Mr. Taylor admits that Hitler was forced to fight the West "before he conquered the East" he admits that he wanted to conquer
the East. Having gone this far he might have turned on Western
Europe and the world—no one can tell—but what we can be sure

of is that he was determined to get possession of Eastern Europe and "to conquer the East" and to persuade or force France and Great Britain to let him do so. Make no doubt of it, Mr. Taylor is clear that Hitler "intended to use force, or would at any rate threaten to use it," at least thus far. He adds that he was a gambler who would play for high stakes with inadequate resources. He even admits at the end that "Hitler may have projected a great war all along."

It is, once again, despite all this good sense that Mr. Taylor dwells not on Hitler's aims or on his policy or even on his "projections" in his discussion of the crises, but only on Hitler's lack of precise plans. He has previously confused plans and policy in his treatment of Bismarck. When he argued that Bismarck never sought a quarrel with France as part of his goal of a united Germany he did so on the ground that Bismarck had no precise plans in 1870; Bismarck stumbled into war and, supreme opportunist that he was, he made the most of it. When new documents proved him wrong about the extent of even Bismarck's planning, let alone about Bismarck's policy and aims, he invented "Taylor's Law"—to the effect that documents do not really signify anything. It is exactly the same with his treatment of Hitler.

The confusion of the occasion with the cause of these crises follows automatically, as does the need to distort the documentary evidence. Because Hitler, like Bismarck, had no precise plans— indeed, it is true of all statesmen that they "are too absorbed by events to follow any preconceived plan"—he did not cause any of these crises. Because somebody must have caused them (for a man who is convinced that statesmen are forever stumbling into decisions, Mr. Taylor has an intense belief that every event flows from somebody's decision, that "the initiative must have come from someone"); "we must look elsewhere for the man who provided an opportunity which Hitler could take and who thus gave the first push (and the subsequent pushes) towards war." In the Austrian crisis it was two men who did this: Von Papen "started Germany's advance towards European domination" by bringing Schuschnigg to see Hitler; Schuschnigg provoked the Anschluss, when Hitler would have preferred to avoid dramatic measures, by deciding on an Austrian plebiscite in defiance of the satellite status that Hitler had already imposed on him. The Anschluss was "the first step in the policy which was to brand [Hitler] as the greatest war criminals. Yet he took this step unintentionally." And because the Hossbach memorandum of November 1937 was not a concrete plan—because it reveals only that Hitler was determined to have Czechoslovakia and Austria, that he hoped to get them without a war, but that he did not know precisely when and how he would get them—it must be explained away.

It was a manoeuvre "in domestic affairs." Mr. Taylor can seriously maintain that its purpose was to win over conservative generals and diplomats to the policy of continued and increased rearmament after showing that Hitler's address was largely devoted to assuring them that Germany would gain her aims without war. In any case it was only "day-dreaming." The whole truth is never to be gleaned from documents. Not all documents mean what they say or what we think they say. But the historian of all people should hesitate before according quite such cavalier treatment to what is at least one of his tools.

It is the same with every subsequent crisis. In every case it was somebody else who caused it. In some cases, as in the Munich crisis, it was everybody else: the German nationalist minority, whom Hitler did not create; the British Government, which was alert to the danger long before Hitler had even formulated his intentions; Lord Runciman, who made appeasement unpopular among the English and thus "helped to clear the way for world war;" the French, for allowing Hitler to overestimate their strength, and the Italians, for allowing him to overestimate their aggressiveness, since otherwise he could have obtained Czechoslovakia—as he hoped to obtain it—without risk in the course of a Franco-Italian war. Hitler only wanted to liberate the Germans in Czechoslovakia and Poland—and to remove the obstacle that Czechoslovakia and Poland presented to German hegemony. Because he did not want to do this by frontal assault and war, because he "preferred the methods of intrigue and violence," because he waited for somebody else to provide him with the opportunity to succeed with these methods, because—above all— he did not have advance plans but waited "without knowing how he would emerge victorious"—for all these reasons he was not responsible for any of the crises.

For the same reason that he did not intend war and hoped to

avoid it he was not responsible in the last crisis for world war: it was "against all expectations" that "he found himself at war with the West before he had conquered the East," "it seems from the record that he became involved in war through launching on 29 August a diplomatic manoeuvre that he ought to have launched on 28 August." The literalism, the inverted subtlety, of the whole approach would be risible if its implications were not so serious.

The implications are serious not only because of their bearing on our understanding of the Second World War. They reduce our possibilities of understanding the causes of war in general. Mr. Taylor's version of the pre-war crises is devoid of all regard for the policy of the man who almost wholly caused them on one level because of his confusion of plans with policy and of occasion with cause. But it also takes this course because the antithesis he has drawn between the profound causes of war and the specific events that lead to war is a false antithesis. It cannot be too much emphasized that, while the profound causes lie in the given conditions that invite war, the causes on the other level are not simply events. They are the ways in which men handle events, react to the challenge which the given conditions present to them. To return once again to the road-accident analogy, it is not to mechanical defects but to the conduct of the driver that we must pay attention when studying a particular collision, and if a road accident can take place independently of the conduct of the driver then a war is not like a road accident. A war is always an alternative to some other course and is always known to be so.

So much is this the case that the relationship between the given conditions and the policy of statesmen, between the profound causes of war and the decisions that lead to war, is not a constant and mechanical relationship as the road-accident analogy would imply. One war may be almost entirely due to the given conditions and hardly at all the consequence of the conduct of the men involved. Another war may be almost entirely due to that conduct and hardly at all the consequence of the given conditions. It is not enough to state that in every case both levels of inquiry exist. It is necessary in each case to discover the relative weight that should be attached to the two levels of causation.

It is for this reason that it must be regretted that Mr. Taylor's analysis of these crises is insulated not only from all regard for the policy of the man who almost wholly caused them on one level but also, as was established earlier, from all recollection of the extreme international unbalance that was the chief cause for them on the other. For only when the crises are studied in this, their proper, context does it emerge to what a large extent the man was responsible, and to what a small extent the conditions, for the outbreak of the Second World War.

Both factors were involved. The unbalance was in a sense the cause of Hitler's policy. If it had not existed and if he had not known that it existed he would not have seen so continuously a "chance of winning" so much. Because he knew it existed he remained confident until the summer of 1939 that he would achieve his aims without war and was thus content in each crisis, as Mr. Taylor never tires of telling us, to wait for the opportunity of doing so. The unbalance was in a sense the cause of the war. Because Hitler's policy succeeded in the reoccupation of the Rhineland, in the Anschluss, in the Munich crisis, in the occupation of Prague he could feel that it would go on succeeding. Because the unbalance was so great it was not easy for other powers to convince him that it would not. The unbalance was so much the cause of Hitler's policy, that anyone else in power in Germany might have had a policy similar to Hitler's, at least in its objects. It was so much the cause of war that, while it was practically impossible for other powers to resist Germany's revisionist attitude up to and including the Munich crisis and equally impossible that they should not resist it if it were persisted in beyond that point, it set up the danger that it would be so persisted in. But it does not advance the cause of historical truth to assert that Hitler was not responsible because somebody else might have pursued the same course; or to assume that somebody else must have pursued the same course beyond the Munich crisis, when the risks had become so great. Mr. Taylor admits this when he says that, although Hitler was no more wicked than many other contemporary statesmen, "in wicked acts he outdid them all." What we do know is that Hitler did pursue it beyond this point. And what we can conclude from any objective analysis of the pre-war crises is that it was this fact, not the unbalance itself, that caused the war.

Neither the *Anschluss*, nor Munich, nor Prague made war inevitable, any more than the reoccupation of the Rhineland had made war inevitable, but with each succeeding crisis the international system creaked a little more stiffly. It is after all a system and, however unbalanced it may be, it will respond to pressure in the end. Mr. Taylor partly recognizes this. In the Polish crisis, he notes, "in strange contrast to earlier crises, there were no negotiations over Danzig, no attempts to discover the solution; not even attempts to screw up tension." Although Hitler went on feeling that he could make it do his work, he felt this with declining confidence, and yet with increasing determination to put the matter to test. Mr. Taylor concedes this too. "There could be no half-hearted German aid to Danzig, only a full-blown war; and Hitler would be ready for such a war only when his military preparation matured." What he conceals is that throughout the last, the Polish crisis, Hitler's confidence was lower, his determination higher, than they had ever been. It is only by maltreating a mass of documentary evidence that he can say that it was "against all expectations that he found himself at war" as the result of this crisis. The most that the evidence will allow us to say is that he involved himself and Europe in war in spite of all his hopes—and because of his refusal to modify the policy of exploiting the unbalance for his ends.

It has been Mr. Taylor's object to shake this widely accepted conclusion. If he was to succeed in this object it was perhaps necessary for him to demonstrate what caused the war if Hitler's policy did not cause it. Has he succeeded in either direction? It is best to answer in his own words. Among the various so-called profound causes for the war which he dismisses is the argument that the war was the inevitable consequence of the existence of "have-not" powers. He replies to it from the field of policy and not from the level of specific events. Insofar as this is another deduction from economic determinism, it was not the economic demands of Germany and Italy that drove them to war—"rather, war or a warlike policy produced the demand for Lebensraum," as for Abyssinia, Corsica, Nice and Savoy. Insofar as it simply means that Hitler and Mussolini had an appetite for success it is an equally worthless explanation of the war: they differed from other statesmen "only in that their appetite was greater, and that they fed it by more unscrupulous means."

10   *G. F. Hudson*
An Apologia for Adolf Hitler

G. F. Hudson is the former Director of the Far Eastern Center of St. Antony's College, Oxford. His major works include Fifty Years of Communism: Theory and Practice, 1917–1967 *(London, 1968).*

It was inevitable that sooner or later some historian should produce a serious apologia for Hitler. This has now arrived, but not from Germany, where the aftermath of the Third Reich is still too painful for such a performance to be acceptable from any personage of academic standing. From the British historian, Mr. A. J. P. Taylor, however, we have in his newly published book, *The Origins of the Second World War,* an interpretation which frankly aims at challenging what he calls "the almost universal agreement among historians" that Hitler "planned the Second World War" and that "his will alone caused it." Mr. Taylor points out that there has been controversy about the origins of the war of 1914; study of the documentary evidence which became so abundant after its close produced a picture of pre-war international politics substantially different from that of Allied wartime "innocentism," and there was wide scope for differences of opinion about the responsibilities of the statesmen principally concerned. For the war of 1939, on the other hand, the captured minutes of Hitler's secret conferences produced at the Nuremberg Trial, and particularly the so-called Hossbach Memorandum of November 1937, appeared to prove on the part of Hitler a def-

SOURCE. G. F. Hudson, "An Apologia for Adolf Hitler," *Commentary.* Copyright © 1962 by the American Jewish Committee. Reprinted by permission of the publisher and author.

inite plan for obtaining supremacy in Europe through a series of acts of military aggression. His responsibility for bringing on a European war in 1939 was therefore considered to be beyond question, and if blame was also cast on the leaders of the Western democracies, it was not for provoking Hitler, but for appeasing him and for failing to stop his career of treaty violation and conquest while it could still have been done without a mortal struggle.

Mr. Taylor, however, questions the conception of Hitler and his policy which is implied in this view. According to him, Hitler's foreign policy "was that of his predecessors" in the German government; he, too, "wanted to free Germany from the restrictions of the peace treaty; to restore a great German army; and then to make Germany the greatest power in Europe from her natural weight." Further, Mr. Taylor denies that Hitler had any preconceived plan or blueprint of conquest on the general argument that "statesmen are too absorbed by events to follow a preconceived plan—the systems attributed to Hitler are really those of Hugh Trevor-Roper, Elizabeth Wiskemann, and Alan Bullock." Finally, Mr. Taylor claims that Hitler always wanted to avoid war, although he was ready to threaten it in order to get his way, and that he did not really want territorial expansion, but only a zone of friendly satellite states in Eastern Europe. His orders to the German army after Munich to be ready to take over Bohemia and Moravia were "measures of precaution, not plans for aggression;" he "doubted whether the [Munich] settlement would work" and "believed, without sinister intention, that independent Czechoslovakia could not survive." There was not "anything sinister or premeditated in the protectorate over Bohemia." In 1939 the state of German armaments "gives the decisive proof that Hitler was not contemplating general war and probably not intending war at all. . . . The war of 1939, far from being premeditated, was a mistake, the result on both sides of diplomatic blunders."

This onslaught on accepted beliefs, coming as it did from a writer with a high reputation as a diplomatic historian, was received by the critics in Britain with a remarkable degree of respect and approval. In particular, *The Times Literary Supplement,* generally regarded as the most important London organ of book reviewing, gave it unqualified praise and spoke of its "impeccable logic." It has naturally been translated into German and is providing an armory of propaganda for those Germans who regard Hitler's Reich as the deeply wronged victim of the Second World War. It has not, however, gone entirely unchallenged; the (anonymous) review in *The Times Literary Supplement* drew several letters of protest from persons well qualified to speak on modern German history, and a full-scale attack on the book was delivered by H. R. Trevor-Roper, the Professor of Modern History in Mr. Taylor's own university. This led to an appearance of the two historians together on the television screen, a medium in which Mr. Taylor has long been established as a star; his performance on this occasion, though technically accomplished, does not appear to have carried conviction with the majority of viewers. Most Englishmen in fact still believe that they were right in opposing Hitler in 1939, and it will take more than Mr. Taylor's "impeccable logic" to persuade them to the contrary, at any rate as long as there is someone else in the picture to point out the inconsistencies and fallacies in his argument.

The book indeed is not one to be dismissed simply with broad generalizations; it can only be refuted by an examination of the evidence to which Mr. Taylor himself appeals. He claims to be an impartial historian whose conclusions have been forced upon him by a study of the documents. "I am concerned to understand what happened," he writes, "not to vindicate or condemn." The critic who observes the manner in which Mr. Taylor selects the material which suits his argument may doubt whether he indeed approaches his theme without bias—especially if he compares Mr. Taylor's conclusions on Hitler with his postwar attitude toward the policies of another totalitarian regime—but it would be going too far afield to inquire into the preconceptions of his peculiar outlook; the primary question is simply whether the picture of Hitler which he presents is one that should be accepted as historically true.

In search of the historical Hitler we have to turn first of all to the pages of *Mein Kampf*. It is true that it was written in 1924–25, and that conditions in Europe had changed by 1933, and even more by 1939. But what Hitler has to say about his ultimate objectives, particularly in Chapter XIV of the second volume, can be compared with Hitler's subsequent actions as ruler of Germany as well as with his statements of policy in the secret directives given to his generals. The most significant passages of this chapter have often been quoted, but it seems worthwhile to quote them again since Mr. Taylor chooses to ignore them. After denouncing the foreign policy of Germany before 1914 because "instead of a sound policy of territorial expansion in Europe" it "embarked on a policy of colonial and trade expansion," Hitler expounds his doctrine of *Lebensraum*. There can only be a "healthy proportion" between a people and its territory if "the support of the people is guaranteed by the resources of its own soil and subsoil." It must, in other words, be virtually autarchic and immune to blockade, and it must have room for a maximum increase of population without losing any by emigration or becoming dependent on imported food. To be a Great Power, with the potentiality of being the strongest of all, Germany must acquire new territory on a grand scale. England, declares Hitler, should not be regarded as a nation which is powerful in spite of the smallness of its territory, "for the English motherland is in reality the great metropolis of the British Empire which owns almost a fourth of the earth's surface. Next to this we must consider the United States as one of the foremost among the colossal states, also Russia and China." In pursuit of a similar territorial magnitude "we National Socialists have purposely drawn a line through the course followed by the prewar Germany in foreign policy. We put an end to the perpetual Germanic march toward the South and West of Europe and turn our eyes toward the lands of the East. We finally put a stop to the colonial and trade policy of prewar times and pass over to the territorial policy of the future. When we speak of new territory in Europe today, we must principally think of Russia and the border states subject to her."

Whatever may be thought of this objective on moral grounds, it is at any rate quite clearly formulated, and it was an aim which Hitler came near to attaining when his armies reached the Neva and the Volga. To say that it was nothing but a continuation of the foreign policy of previous German governments is quite untrue. There had for a long time been elements in Germany which had nursed such ideas, but they had certainly not been motives of official German policy before 1914; the vast gains of the Brest-

Litovsk Treaty had been the outcome of Russia's wartime collapse in 1917, not of any prewar scheme for the conquest of Russia. Under the Weimar Republic we cannot assign such projects of territorial expansion to a Rathenau, a Stresemann, or a Bruening. In fact, Hitler complains that his aims for the future of Germany were rejected, not only by liberals and pacifists, who were prepared to submit to the restrictions of the Treaty of Versailles, but also by the nationalists, whose purposes were confined to recovering for the Reich the frontiers of 1914. What Hitler proposes is a territory on which 250 million Germans can be self-supporting in a hundred years' time. He is quite clear that this territory can only be taken from other nations, and declares plainly that "our people will not obtain territory, and therewith the means of existence, as a favor from any other people but will have to win it by the power of a triumphant sword."

Twelve years after writing this as the leader of a small political party which had failed ignominiously in an attempt at a *coup d'état* in Bavaria, Hitler held forth on the same theme to the heads of the German armed forces who listened to him as their Fuehrer, and declared: "The history of all times has proved that space expansion can only be effected by breaking resistance and taking risks. Even setbacks are unavoidable; neither formerly nor today has space been found without an owner. The question for Germany is where the greatest possible conquest could be made at the lowest cost."

Mr. Taylor dismisses the minutes of these secret conferences as convincing evidence of Hitler's intentions on the ground that Hitler would not wish to reveal his inmost thoughts to his generals, whom he distrusted. This point may be conceded, but its implication is just the opposite of what Mr. Taylor requires for his case. He suggests that Hitler simply ranted and talked big in front of his generals, going far beyond what he really intended to do. But Hitler's relations with the heads of armed forces and the circumstances of his speeches make it likely that he told them, not more, but less than he had it in his mind to do in the long run. He was not talking to beer-hall cronies who would be impressed by empty fantasies of empire-building, but to professional military men who, on the one hand, would have the duty of carrying out whatever he required of them for the execution of his policies, but on the other hand were openly alarmed lest Germany's strength should be overstrained by projects too vast for her undertaking. Tactically it was in Hitler's interest to instruct them at each stage in what he wanted of them without alarming them too much by premature revelation of the total design. Above all, it was not expedient in November 1937 to set before the generals the conquest of Russia as an ultimate objective of policy, for the principle of good relations with Russia in Germany's weakened condition after 1918 had become an article of faith with the Reichswehr and had the authority of Bismarckian tradition behind it. So there is nothing about attacking Russia in the Hossbach Memorandum; the immediate program of aggression is limited to Austria and Czechoslovakia. Only after the conclusion of the Nazi-Soviet Pact do we find Hitler declaring to his commanders at Obersalzberg on August 22, 1939: "My pact with Poland [of 1934] was only meant to gain time. And with Russia will happen just what I have done in Poland. After Stalin's death —we shall crush the Soviet Union." But this was not really anything new; it was already there in *Mein Kampf*. The curious qualification "after Stalin's death" was perhaps due to a feeling that some regard should be paid at least in words to the man with whom he had just concluded a treaty of mutual nonaggression.

With regard to Austria and Czechoslovakia, the Hossbach Memorandum shows Hitler as saying after a discussion of the conditions for successful attacks on both countries: "The annexation of the two states to Germany, militarily and politically, would constitute a considerable relief, owing to shorter and better frontiers, the freeing of fighting personnel for other purposes, and the possibility of constituting new armies up to a strength of twelve divisions." In this policy statement, made three months before the *Anschluss* and ten before Munich, it should be noticed that both countries are to be fully annexed and there is no question of taking merely the Sudetenland without the rest of Bohemia and Moravia. Mr. Taylor, nevertheless, treats the incorporation of Austria in the Reich as an afterthought to an invasion which Hitler had not previously intended. It is not true, as Mr. Taylor claims, that the timing of the move against Austria was determined by Schuschnigg's coup of a snap plebiscite on Austrian independence, which would have been a serious political setback for Hitler if he had permitted it to take place, but this does not mean that the absorption of Austria at an appropriate time had not already been planned by Hitler, as the Hossbach Memorandum shows that it was.

The Hossbach Memorandum also provides the key to an understanding of the Munich crisis. The paradox of that episode is that Germany and all the world saw in it a great triumph for Hitler because he got the Sudetenland, whereas Hitler was in a fury because he had been deprived of his entry into Prague. In order to neutralize Britain, where Chamberlain was known to be in favor of a cession of the Sudetenland to Germany on ethnic grounds, Hitler picked his quarrel with Czechoslovakia on the Sudeten question, but this was to be the pretext for a war against Czechoslovakia in which Hitler believed that Britain and France would stand aside and the whole of Bohemia would be overrun. But Chamberlain persuaded the French to join with him in putting pressure on the Czechs to cede the Sudetenland, and their submission deprived Hitler of his pretext; when he put up his terms at Godesberg, he found the British attitude becoming tougher, and finally there was the mobilization of the British fleet. Hitler called off the war and accepted the Munich agreement which gave him the Sudetenland, but not the predominantly Czech areas of Bohemia. Immediately afterward he ordered the German army to get ready for the occupation of the Czech lands and he carried out the takeover in March of 1939. Thus the conquests projected in the Hossbach Memorandum were completed. But Mr. Taylor will not allow that Hitler had ever intended to go to Prague or that he had good strategic and economic reasons for doing so. "He did it without design," writes Mr. Taylor, ignoring the plain words of the Hossbach Memorandum; "it brought him slight advantage. He acted only when events had already destroyed the settlement of Munich." Mr. Taylor holds that the disturbances in Slovakia early in March took Hitler by surprise, but there is substantial evidence that these troubles, although arising out of a genuine Slovak nationalism, were fomented from Berlin.

When five months later the crisis between Germany and Poland came to a head, Mr. Taylor accepts the German thesis that it was about Danzig. Indeed he heads the last chapter of his book "War for Danzig," and the title is not meant to be ironical. Danzig was chosen as the issue because the German ethnic character of its population made it possible to invoke the principle of nationality. But to his generals on May 23 Hitler declared: "The Pole is no 'supplementary enemy.' Poland will always be on the side of our adversaries. . . . Danzig is not the subject of the dispute at all. It is a question of expanding our living space in the East. . . . Poland sees danger in a German victory in the West and will attempt to rob us of that victory. There is therefore no question of sparing Poland and we are left with the decision: to attack Poland at the first suitable opportunity. . . . We cannot expect a repetition of the Czech affair. There will be war."

That should be clear enough, especially as these were not words spoken in casual conversation, but an address to the heads of the armed forces charged with the military preparations for the attack, which as a matter of history actually took place on the date assigned for it. The intention is not, however, clear enough for Mr. Taylor, who, as we have seen, considers that "the war of 1939, far from being premeditated, was a mistake, the result on both sides of diplomatic blunders." But it is hard to see where the blunders came in, given the fact of the British and French guarantees to Poland. Both Britain and France were pledged to come to the aid of Poland if she were attacked; Germany deliberately attacked Poland, and Britain and France went to war—though with minimum effort—in accordance with their pledges. Everybody acted with their eyes open and there was no misunderstanding. It is regarded by some people as a blunder that Britain should have given a guarantee to Poland at all without prior agreement with Russia and thereafter should have pursued negotiations for an alliance with Russia in such a dilatory fashion. But the guarantee was originally given without any idea of making it conditional on Russian backing, and failure to get a Russian alliance was not in the eyes of the British government any reason for going back on the guarantee. Hitler hoped, as the record of his speech of May 23 shows, that his coup de théâtre of a pact with Stalin—which he knew he could make whenever he wanted it on the basis of a partition of Poland and the Baltic States with Russia—might deter Britain and France from intervening, but the same speech shows that he did not count on it and was determined to go through with his attack even if they did intervene. In other words, he conditionally willed a European war of which he had formal and solemn warning, and he can no more be said to have tried to avoid war than a bandit who shoots a bank cashier can be held innocent of murder because he hoped that his victim might hand over the cash without resisting.

Mr. Taylor evidently thinks the Poles ought to have capitulated; "sober statesmen," he says, "would have surrendered at discretion when they contemplated the dangers threatening Poland and the inadequacy of her means." In support of his disapproval he is able to quote Nevile Henderson as saying, "I have held from the beginning that the Poles were utterly foolish and unwise" and the American Ambassador's report to Washington that Chamberlain was "more worried about getting the Poles to be reasonable than the Germans." But Britain was pledged to assist Poland "if any action were taken which clearly threatened their independence and which the Polish government accordingly felt obliged to resist with their national forces;" there was no condition that the Poles must be "reasonable" by making unilateral concessions to German demands. The criticism must, therefore, refer back to the original British guarantee, and it is indeed for this that Mr. Taylor reserves his most biting denunciation. He makes great play with the record that when the Polish foreign minister was informed of the proposed British guarantee, he accepted it "between two flicks of ash off his cigarette." "Two flicks," writes Mr. Taylor, "and British grenadiers would die for Danzig. Two flicks; and the illusory great Poland, created in 1919, signed her death-warrant." But let us suppose that there had been no offer of guarantee, that Britain in March 1939 had decided to let events in Eastern Europe take their course. In all probability Poland would then have capitulated to Germany and accepted the proposals for an offensive alliance against Russia which we know from the published Polish documents had been repeatedly offered to her. It can be argued that Poland would thus have been better off; at any rate, her ultimate fate as an ally of Germany could hardly have been worse than it was to be as an ally of Britain. But what of Britain and France? We may let Hitler speak for himself, even though it was only to his generals; in his speech of August 22, he said: "I thought I would turn first against the West and

only afterward against the East. But the sequence cannot be fixed.
. . . I wanted to establish an acceptable relationship with Poland
in order to fight first against the West, but this plan, which was
agreeable to me, could not be executed. It became clear to me
that Poland would attack us in case of conflict with the West."

Hitler's claim is that, having made his nonaggression pact with
Poland in 1934, he had hoped for a pro-German trend of Polish
policy which would have enabled him to count on Polish neutrality in a German war with Britain and France, but since Poland
had accepted a British guarantee and revived her alliance with
France, the destruction of Poland must be the primary objective;
quick decision because of the season." But why had Hitler been
thinking about war in the West even if Poland had become a
German satellite and there had been no British guarantee of her
independence? The answer is given in the Hossbach Memorandum: "German policy must reckon with its two hateful enemies,
England and France, to whom a strong German colossus in the
center of Europe would be intolerable." Hitler indeed reckoned,
and as the event showed, rightly, that however long it might take
for Britain and France to make up their minds to oppose the expansion of Germany, they would ultimately do so. He knew their
desire for peace and was ready to exploit it to the full in the early
stages of his policy, but unless they were definitely willing to
renounce all concern with the affairs of Eastern Europe and even
to join him in a war against Russia, he could not count on their
benevolent neutrality for the final and decisive phase of his design. They might strike at him or impose an armed mediation at
the moment when his armies were committed in the interior of
Russia; when the prospect of a Germany extending from the
Rhine to the Volga was revealed before their eyes, they would
deem it too dangerous to be tolerated. Logically, therefore, they
must be attacked and crushed before the conquest of Russia could
be undertaken. In his speech to his generals of May 23, Hitler
speculated on the chances of a surprise attack on the British fleet,
but added that it would only be possible if Germany were not
involved in war with Britain on account of Poland, i.e., if Germany were able to choose the moment to strike in time of peace
without declaration of war. The valid inference is that if Britain
had failed to go to war on behalf of Poland, she would have been

subjected to a "Pearl Harbor" attack shortly afterward, and it is highly unlikely that she would have survived it.

But Mr. Taylor will have none of this. Hitler only wanted "a free hand to destroy conditions in the East which enlightened Western opinion had also pronounced intolerable" and he "had no ambitions directed against Great Britain and France." What a pity indeed that we did not let this admirable German states-man have his way! We should not then have this tiresome post-war situation which now confronts us. But many of us would no longer be here to be confronted with anything; in company probably with Mr. Taylor himself we should long ago have perished in Buchenwald or Dachau.

11   *A. L. Rowse*
Beneath the Whitewash the Same Old Hitler

A. L. Rowse, the author of distinguished works on Elizabethan England, has also written Appeasement: A Study in Political Decline, 1933–39, *which was published almost at the same time as the* Origins.

It is well known that this book has been the subject of acute and heated controversy in Britain, and is probably explosive matter for a reviewer to touch. When it first appeared last April, it was hailed by a chorus of praise from ingenuous publicists who knew little about the subject and had no faculty for criticism; on the second wave, it was subjected to scarifying comment by authorities who knew what they were talking about. The book was given the most devastating analysis that I have ever seen by H. R. Trevor-Roper in *Encounter*, leaving the author with not a

SOURCE. A. L. Rowse, "Beneath the Whitewash the Same Old Hitler," *The New York Times*, Jan. 7, 1962. Copyright © 1962 by *The New York Times*. Reprinted by permission.

leg to stand on. No serious attempt was made, since none was possible, to meet the criticisms; and now the book is published in the United States with no changes, so far as I can see, except for a "Preface for the American Reader."

A. J. P. Taylor is the *enfant terrible* of English intellectual and journalistic life. He is an Oxford don, regarded as a stimulating, provocative teacher. As a political figure, he is a man of the extreme Left, very much to the fore in the unilateral Disarmament Campaign, though he combines this with writing regularly for the Beaverbrook press, for which he signalized himself by advocating the ending of the United Nations. In addition, he is a television performer of the first magnitude, with a vast audience.

Now, for the historian, the prime necessity is for accuracy of statement: one must be able to rely on what the man says, or he is not any good as a historian. Almost equally necessary is responsibility of judgment.

Mr. Taylor's "Preface for the American Reader" contains a good many trenchant strictures on American policy before the war, and then says, "The general moral of this book, so far as it has one, is that Great Britain and France dithered between resistance and appeasement, and so helped to make war more likely. American policy did much the same." There is something in that, of course; but it is putting the cart before the horse. As if this were the primary cause of the war! The *primary* cause, as we all know, was Hitler's dynamic drive towards world power—to which Britain and France were merely reacting, insufficiently strongly.

Mr. Taylor, however, makes his fortune by calling in question what we all know and going flat against common sense. He practically tells us that Hitler was not responsible for the war; then he, too, dithers and concludes, not until the last page, that "Hitler *may* have projected a great war all along." But there is no doubt what the book adds up to: by way of originality, out to affront, to shock, rather than to seek the truth and insure it, it is a whitewashing of Hitler.

We are told, "in principle and doctrine, Hitler was no more wicked and unscrupulous than many other contemporary statesmen. In wicked acts he outdid them all." This is an entirely false disjunction. If a political leader inseminates and enforces the wicked racial rubbish of anti-Semitism, it will come to be carried out. But this historian lets Hitler off. He says, "Everything which Hitler did against the Jews followed logically from the racial doctrines in which most Germans vaguely believed." Here is another simple confusion of thought: whatever nonsense people may think, one must make a distinction between those who have not committed murder, and those who in fact have—and mass murders on a terrible scale too.

This overwhelming fact is hardly mentioned throughout the length of Mr. Taylor's book. It might be pleaded that there is a technical reason for this: that this is diplomatic history, concerned with the foreign relations of the powers and their documentation. If that is so, then this is unilateral history, history in only one dimension, with the whole heart, soul and substance of the matter left out. How can one hope to understand or explain what happened by merely reading the surface of things in the diplomatic notes the powers exchanged with one another and without taking into account the full nature of the Nazi regime in all its barbarity? What is the point of it? What value is there in it?

Even so, Mr. Taylor is at pains to whittle down Hitler's responsibility at every point. In the English edition, he gave the game away by saying that his is "a story without heroes, and perhaps even without villains." In both editions, speaking as a politician, I suppose, he tells us that putting the blame on Hitler "satisfied the Germans, except for a few unrepentant Nazis." Another half-truth. Again and again we are told that it was not Hitler who made this crisis or that, others did it for him. Over Czechoslovakia, "even more than in the case of Austria, Hitler did not need to act. Others would do his work for him. The crisis over Czechoslovakia was provided for Hitler. He merely took advantage of it."

He tells us with regard to Munich, that "the settlement at Munich was a triumph for British policy, which has worked precisely to this end; not a triumph for Hitler, who had started with no such clear intention." This is in complete contradiction to Sir Winston Churchill, who stated at the time that it was one of the gravest defeats that British policy had ever suffered.

Mr. Taylor is very cocksure in his certainty as to Hitler's intentions: he might just have looked at the evidence plain for all to see in "Mein Kampf." There we can see the objective made clear: *Lebensraum* in Eastern Europe, room for a population of 250 million Germans, a war of conquest against Russia, a German Army strong enough to achieve it and overthrow the West if necessary. He meant what he said, no political leader more so. Why deny the plain facts to titillate the gallery?

There is a simple intellectual confusion here also: that between strategy and tactics. Of course, Hitler was flexible as to tactics, prepared to wait for opportunities to come along and exploit them, but that does not mean that there was not a grand strategy as to which he was inflexible, with an overriding objective: the domination of Europe. Mr. Taylor admits as much in passing, for his book is as full of self-contradictions as of misstatements.

One of the more innocent publicists in England greeted the book as "a flawless masterpiece;" it is, in fact, flawed from top to bottom and offers an exemplary instance how history should not be written. . . . Mr. Taylor's writings on World War II include the book, "Sword and Swastika."

12   *W. N. Medlicott*
in The English Historical Review

Professor Emeritus Medlicott, of the London School of Economics, is the author of British Foreign Policy Since Versailles *and other prominent works in diplomatic history.*

Starting from the assumption that "the greatest masters of statecraft are those who do not know what they are doing," Mr. A. J. P. Taylor in *The Origins of the Second World War* (Lon-

SOURCE. Reprinted with permission of the author and *The English Historical Review*.

don: Hamish Hamilton, 1961) attributes the success of Adolf
Hitler's earlier foreign policy to his mastery "in the game of
waiting," and after the Munich agreement Hitler was, he argues,
again merely waiting for events to provide him with success.
Speaking of this period he insists that there is not "the smallest
fragment of evidence" that Hitler ever considered plans for attack
on the Western Powers "even in the most remote way"; he was
taken by surprise by the Slovak quarrel with the Czechs and occupied Prague on 15 March 1939 only to defend Slovakia from
the Hungarians; no plan for the annexation of Memel can be
found in the records. Unfortunately for Mr. Taylor's argument
there is contrary evidence on all these points. In the published
German documents we find directions from Hitler to the *Wehr-
macht* on 21 October 1938 to be prepared for the occupation of
Memel; there is a plan, drawn up by Keitel on Hitler's detailed
instructions and dated 26 November 1938, for a German-Italian
attack on France and England; and instructions to prepare for
the "liquidation of the Rump Czech State" were issued by Hitler
on 17 December 1938. However, it appears from Mr. Taylor's
account that when the war came no one was more taken aback
than Hitler; far from being premeditated it was a mistake, "the
result on both sides of diplomatic blunders." I hope I have stated
the gist of Mr. Taylor's argument fairly. He puts his case against
Hitler's premeditation somewhat tentatively: "this is a rival
dogma which is worth developing, if only as an academic exercise." Two arguments that support his case up to a point are the
willingness of France and England to remove Germany's real or
alleged grievances under the Versailles treaty, and the fact that
Germany was less well prepared for a major war in 1939 than she
would be when her rearmament programme was completed in
1943 or 1944. But all this does not prove that Hitler was "probably not intending war at all" in 1939, or that it only occurred
to him in the summer of 1939 that it would be profitable to fight
while Germany was relatively stronger than her opponents (in any
case the two arguments seem to be contradictory). The idea that
the clever thing might be to fight France and England in 1938
or 1939 is set out clearly enough in the Hossbach minutes of 10
November 1937. It is really impossible to see Hitler in the documentation for 1939 as other than hard at work to secure his war

(or the fruits of victory without war) as expeditiously as possible. Mr. Taylor is extraordinarily reluctant to recognize or remind himself of the more dynamic and explosive sides of Hitler's character. This is a readable but somewhat baffling and unconvincing book; if there is a Hitler problem Mr. Taylor has not solved it.

13   *Louis Morton*
From Fort Sumter To Poland
The Question of War Guilt

Louis Morton is Professor of History at Dartmouth College and specializes in military history. His works include a volume of the United States official history of World War II, Strategy and Command *(Washington, 1962).*

I

It is now more than a hundred years since the first shot was fired at Fort Sumter in Charleston Harbor, precipitating four years of terrible conflict. Since then, the question of who was responsible for the opening salvo of the Civil War has continued to occupy the attention of publicists, polemicists, politicians, and scholars.

There is no doubt about who fired the first shot; it was the Confederate battery across the channel from Sumter at Fort Johnson. The exact time—4:30 A.M., April 12, 1861—and the circumstances surrounding that event are known almost to the last detail. Nor did Jefferson Davis ever seek to evade or deny his responsibility for the decision that led to the bombardment. But this admission is only the beginning of any inquiry into the ques-

SOURCE. Louis Morton, "From Fort Sumter to Poland The Question of War Guilt," *World Politics,* Jan. 1962, Vol. XIV, No. 2, pp. 386–392. Copyright © 1962 by Princeton University Press. Reprinted by permission.

tion of responsibility. Davis contended then and later that the order to fire on Fort Sumter was necessary as a measure of defense; that Lincoln had provoked the conflict by his refusal to evacuate the fort in Charleston Harbor, the very heart of the Confederacy, and that his effort to send provisions to Major Anderson at Sumter constituted an open act of aggression.

Lincoln supporters deny the charge, but not the facts. The President, they say, was simply trying to maintain the *status quo*. He had promised to send only food to the Sumter garrison, which was nearing the end of its supply, and in doing this he was merely doing his duty as President. He meant to preserve the Union and protect Federal property, but he did not seek war. The choice was the South's, and it made its choice on the morning of April 12, 1861.

Here we have posed sharply the difficult problem of responsibility for the Civil War. There is no question that Lincoln by his decision to send provisions to Fort Sumter presented Davis with a hard choice. Did he do so deliberately to provoke the Confederate leader into firing at Sumter, or was he genuinely seeking to preserve the peace while maintaining the form but not the substance of Federal authority? Did Jefferson Davis actively desire war as the only means to consolidate Confederate sentiment in the South and bring Virginia and the wavering border states into the Confederacy? Did Lincoln's effort to feed the starving garrison furnish Davis, therefore, with the pretext he needed to start a war that would save the infant Confederacy?

The arguments on both sides have been repeated endlessly. After a century of historical study, the facts are clear; they have been recounted at considerable length over and over again. The differences are differences in emphasis and interpretation, and it is about these that the debate continues. The fact is that Lincoln and Davis were in much the same position in April 1861. Each wanted peace on his own terms, Southern Independence or Union. The issue had been put by Webster a decade earlier when he said in his much quoted Seventh of March speech that peaceable secession was an utter impossibility, politically and morally. Given Lincoln's determination to preserve the Union, the South could only hope to achieve independence by force. Even if there had been no Sumter, Lincoln would have had to take some sort of

action. Northern sentiment demanded it and the future of the
nation depended upon it.

Davis was as determined on independence as Lincoln was on
union. So long as the North refused to recognize the Confederacy
as an independent nation and maintained forts in the South, his
position was untenable. It was rendered more so by Unionist
sentiment in the South and by the failure of the border states to
come over to his side.

By early April, if not before, war had become inevitable. For
Davis there was no turning back; for Lincoln no compromise with
union. Both men faced extremists who threatened to take the
initiative into their own hands; both calculated the risks of delay.
Action would risk war; inaction the cause for which each man
stood. But it was Lincoln, not Davis, who broke the deadlock. For
by his decision to send provisions to Fort Sumter he presented the
Confederate leader with the ultimate choice.

And so we come back to the question that has always plagued
students of the Civil War. What did Lincoln intend when he
ordered the ships to Charleston Harbor? The answer will probably never be known, for it lies buried in the mind of Lincoln,
beyond the reach of curious historians. But there is a larger question here that has broader implications than the guilt of any one
man, and that is: What is the significance of this concern with responsibility for war? Is it purely an historical question or does
it reflect deeper forces and contemporary issues?

II

This question of war guilt is an ever-present theme in American
history and exercises a fatal fascination for historians. Who fired
the first shot at Lexington that lit the tinderbox of the Revolution? Did we go to war with England in 1812 to protect American
sailors at sea from impressment, or were our motives less noble?
Did Polk send General Taylor into disputed territory deliberately
to provoke war with Mexico and thus gain by force what he
could not acquire by peaceful means? Did we join Britain and
France in 1917 to make the world safe from German domination,
to protect the investment of bankers and munitions makers, or
because of British propaganda? Did the sinking of the "Lusitania"
merely furnish the pretext for a decision already made?

World War II provides only the most recent example of this tendency to pin the guilt for war on a single man, actuated by ulterior purposes. The United States had scarcely emerged from that war when revisionist historians began to reexamine the events that had led to Pearl Harbor. The result was strikingly similar to the revisionist view of the attack on Fort Sumter. In its simplest form, the thesis may be stated as follows: President Roosevelt maneuvered Japan into attack by diplomatic and economic pressure, withheld vital information from Admiral Kimmel and General Short, and deliberately kept the Pacific Fleet at Pearl Harbor against the advice of Admiral Richardson to invite attack and so bring the American people into the war united behind the Administration. Pearl Harbor, from this point of view, may be termed President Roosevelt's Sumter.

Even if it was not good history, this interpretation found wide acceptance because it served several purposes. For Roosevelt's political enemies it provided a convenient weapon to use against the late President and his party. Isolationists, who wished to withdraw from the complexities and dangers of leadership in the nuclear age, found in it support for their own views. Anglophobes and pro-German groups took comfort in it, for it affirmed their belief that the United States had been the victim of British deceit and propaganda as in 1917.

In addition to the political and ideological causes it may serve, revisionism reflects a moral concern with the overt act of aggression and a deep-felt need to justify the ultimate resort to force. National interest is not enough to justify war, for in the American view war is justifiable only in self-defense against attack. An open act of aggression, no matter how just the cause, brands the aggressor and fixes the guilt. Thus, the opening blow of the war assumes a significance scarcely warranted in the sequence of events that led to the war. For Americans, therefore, it is a matter of prime importance to believe that the overt act was defensive and not aggressive.

The moral anxiety displayed by Americans toward the use of force has, it would seem, placed the issue of war guilt in a moral rather than a political setting. In the belief that war is evil, no matter what the cause, and that no objective can justify resort to force except in self-defense, American historians have shown infinite patience and endless ingenuity in their efforts to establish responsibility for the first blow. The position of the United States today with regard to preventive and preemptive war illustrates this principle vividly. "Our arms will never be used to strike the first blow in any attack," said President Kennedy in his special message to Congress on the Defense budget in January 1961. ". . . It is our national tradition." And it is not without significance that the present military policy of the United States is to develop and maintain a nuclear *retaliatory* force—i.e., a force capable of striking the enemy after he has hit us first. Or that American strategy, in military parlance, is called a second-strike strategy, as distinguished from a first-strike strategy.

III

Americans are not alone in their concern over the morality of force and responsibility for war. Other nations share this concern and their histories reflect the need for justification, whether on moral, political, or emotional grounds. Certainly the Germans, who were officially branded the aggressors after World War I, viewed the events that led to the war in a different light from the French and British. And when their historians began to write the history of that period, they found the Allies less innocent than had been thought. Some British and American historians began also to revise the existing interpretation of the war, criticizing the policies of their own government and questioning the reasons for going to war. On the German side, there was a practical aspect to this rewriting of history. For if it could be demonstrated that Germany was not guilty of starting the war, then the punitive clauses of the Versailles Treaty could be attacked as unjust as well as unwise. The revisionist historians on the Allied side had their own reasons for challenging the accepted view of Germany's war guilt. Thus, the decade of the 1920's and 1930's witnessed a continuing historical debate over the causes of World War I, a debate conducted in an atmosphere of general disillusion with war and economic depression.

Revisionist writing after World War II was confined to the United States and concerned itself almost exclusively with the events that led to the Japanese attack on Pearl Harbor. The only question was the extent to which President Roosevelt was responsible for America's entry into the war. Responsibility for the war that began in Europe in 1939 received little attention from the revisionists, who, like most historians, accepted the standard interpretation that the conflict was brought on by the egomaniac Hitler with his plan for world conquest—a judgmen that was, or seemed to be, amply confirmed by the mass of evidence accumulated at the Nuremberg Trials.

Fixing the guilt for World War II on Hitler was, in many ways, a most satisfying explanation of the origins of the war, and there was little disposition in the United States or abroad to question it, especially as the prospect of a third and more horrible world war appeared increasingly likely. Hitler's guilt fixed responsibility clearly. It was a simple explanation that could be understood and accepted by everyone. It placed the responsibility on one man, a madman who was now dead and therefore in no position to affirm his innocence. This interpretation also confirmed the immediate prewar policies of the Allied war leaders and concealed any errors of judgment they may have made. It absolved the German people of blame not only for the war but for all the atrocities of the Hitler regime. And it satisfied Germany's former allies because they could claim that Hitler forced them to do what they did. Even the diehard American revisionists could take solace from this thesis, for it explained how the United States had become involved in the European war. No sane German statesman would have declared war on the United States after the Pearl Harbor attack. Only a madman like Hitler could have done so.

This version of events has stood virtually unchallenged from 1939 until this past year when the distinguished and controversial British historian, A. J. P. Taylor, undertook to provide a different explanation of the origins of the war. An authority on modern German history not noted for his sympathetic treatment of the Germans, Professor Taylor asserts that Hitler's war guilt is a myth, that the Nuremberg records are a lawyer's brief and not to be trusted, and that the war was the result very largely of the blunders of Western statesmen. Hitler, according to this interpretation, far from being a madman, was merely a traditional German statesman seeking to restore Germany to its "natural" position in Europe. To do so, he had to destroy the system created at Versailles—a system, says Taylor, that "lacked moral validity from the start," and had no basis in the realities of the European balance of power. Thus, in seeking lost German territory, Hitler was only righting a moral wrong and doing what was politically necessary. He had no long-range plan for war, no blueprint for world conquest. After all, says Taylor, "statesmen are too absorbed by events to follow a preconceived plan. They take one step, and the next step follows from it." And Hitler was no different from other political leaders; he simply took advantage of the "objective" situation in Europe.

In Taylor's interpretation of the events that led to World War II, Hitler is pictured as a passive instrument reacting to external pressures. He did not desire annexation of Austria and Czechoslovakia, or war with Poland. These measures were forced on him by events—the objective situation—and the policies pursued by Germany's enemies. It was Schuschnigg, not Hitler, who provoked the Austrian crisis; the Sudeten Nazis, independent of Hitler, who provoked the Czech crisis; the intransigent Poles who brought on the Polish crisis. The Munich Settlement in Taylor's version was not appeasement but wise recognition of Germany's rightful claim, "a triumph for all that was best and most enlightened in British life." That it did not save Czechoslovakia was not Hitler's fault or Neville Chamberlain's; it was the Czechs who forced Hitler to occupy Prague. Similarly, in the Polish crisis, Hitler wanted merely to right the wrong of Versailles in the matter of Danzig. He sought not war with the Poles, only friendship, and the proof of this, says Taylor, can be found in Germany's inadequate military strength, which in 1939 was far from sufficient to carry out the conquest of Europe. Even the Nazi-Soviet Pact of August 1939, we are told, was intended by Hitler to prevent war, not to prepare for it. But the French and British, acting irrationally, refused to be dissuaded by the pact and gave Poland their support. The war that followed, concludes Taylor, "far from being premeditated, was a mistake, the result on both sides of diplomatic blunders."

This, in brief, is Professor Taylor's thesis. It is powerfully argued, brilliantly written, and always persuasive. Whether it is good history is another matter. Already it has come under a strong attack from some of the most eminent historians in Britain as "utterly erroneous," a distortion of history, a perversion of the evidence, irresponsible and a disgrace to the profession of historian. Most historians will want to weigh the evidence carefully and examine Mr. Taylor's assumptions and methods (which are certainly open to question) before accepting his thesis. In the final analysis, however, the strength of revisionist writing depends less on historical accuracy than on deep-felt needs to explain the past in terms of present problems. Taylor's thesis strikes the same chord and has the same moral and political implications as the revisionist writing after World War I. Germany is no longer the major power of Europe seeking to assert its natural weight in affairs. The Soviet Union has taken its place, and the Germans are now British allies. German troops assigned to NATO are being trained in England and the Berlin crisis raises the possibility of armed intervention on behalf of the Germans. If World War II was a diplomatic blunder for which the Western powers must bear a fair share of the blame, as Taylor says, then perhaps Germany deserves the support of its former enemies. Certainly no one wishes to repeat the blunders of 1939, if indeed, the war was the result of a blunder.

The question of responsibility for World War II has other implications for our own time and Mr. Taylor's volume may mark the beginning of a rewriting of the history of the period preceding the war. Already it has given support to the neo-Nazi movement in Germany and will undoubtedly find a sympathetic hearing among similar groups in other countries, including the United States. One can expect also that the judgment of Nuremberg will be sharply challenged, as was the Versailles verdict after World War I. And if we must revise our picture of Hitler, as Taylor says, then will not the next step be to adjust our image of Stalin, and perhaps also of Khrushchev? If Hitler had no blueprint for conquest (notwithstanding *Mein Kampf* and the Hossbach Memorandum), then, to follow Taylor's reasoning, how much weight should we attach to Khrushchev's claim that he will bury capitalism? If Hitler was only acting under the pressure of events to secure for Germany only what was right and just, may not Khrushchev be taken as merely a Russian version of the German model? How then shall we treat with him? Shall we take his claims of world conquest seriously and oppose him as we did Hitler, and thus, as in 1939, blunder into a world war? Or shall we give him what he asks in the belief that he (like Hitler) is merely a traditional statesman seeking his country's natural rights? In a sense, this is the central question of our time, and the answer to it may depend partly on our reading of history.

14   *Time*

Time's review of the Origins *is typical of the book's reception in the United States.*

Anxious to rescue history from simple moral judgments, historians have been restoring the reputations of many a traditional villain. Richard III, Metternich, Aaron Burr have all been readmitted to civilized society and admired for their "realism." But no one (outside Germany) seemed to have thought of scrubbing up Hitler—until now. In *The Origins of the Second World War*, Oxford Historian A. J. P. Taylor finds excuses for Hitler and reasons to blame nearly everybody else.

Provoked by Little Powers. Most historians have pictured Hitler as a juggernaut. In Taylor's account, he is peculiarly passive. "He did not seize power," writes Taylor, "he waited for it to be thrust upon him." Like other statesmen of his time, he was defending the national interest in a cleanly Machiavellian way. He simply wanted to overturn the Treaty of Versailles and restore Germany as a great power. Minimizing the fact that Hitler committed his plans for conquest to paper as early as 1925 in *Mein Kampf,* Taylor claims that the dictator did not really want war.

SOURCE. This review appeared in *Time* on January 12, 1962. Reprinted by permission from *Time,* The Weekly Newsmagazine; Copyright Time Inc., 1962.

His threats were "daydreaming" or "playacting" to impress German generals who wanted to slow him down.

In Taylor's view, it was always somebody else who put poor, passive Hitler in a mood to fight. "Provoked" by the Austrian Chancellor, Kurt von Schuschnigg, Hitler improvised the invasion of Austria almost overnight, as proved by the fact that 70% of the German transport broke down on the way. When Hitler ordered his generals to "smash" Czechoslovakia, it was merely a "momentary display of temper." The real culprits, Taylor implies, were the men foolhardy enough to stand up to Hitler. Poland's Foreign Minister Jozef Beck had such "great power arrogance" about his little nation that he tricked Britain into the foolish defense pact that started World War II.

Theatrical Destruction. With scholarly detachment, Taylor states the case for appeasing Hitler and for resisting him, but his sympathies obviously lie with the appeasers. Germany, he argues, had a right as a great power to reoccupy the Rhineland in 1936, even though Winston Churchill, among others, felt that Hitler could have been easily stopped and probably toppled from power. At Munich, writes Taylor, British Prime Minister Neville Chamberlain saved the peace and served the principle of self-determination, i.e., by handing a slice of Czechoslovakia to Germany because a lot of Germans lived there. Writes Taylor: "It was a triumph of all that was best and most enlightened in British life."

Taylor insists that Hitler was no fanatic. "Hitler was a rational, though no doubt a wicked statesman," writes Taylor primly. "His object was the steady expansion of German power, not a theatrical display of glory." This is an odd assessment of a man who wallowed in the theatrical, whether haranguing the chanting mobs under the searchlights at Nürnberg or accepting the total destruction of Germany as a suitable Götterdämmerung to accompany his own demise. His nationalism, far from being the common variety, was the most virulent racism the world has ever known.

"A study of history is of no practical use in the present or future," Taylor, who likes to be whimsical, once said. As far as Taylor himself is concerned, his book proves his point.

15   Frank Freidel
                    Who Started The War?

*Frank Freidel is Professor of History at Harvard University,
and the author of several books on the World War II era. His
review article is especially interesting because it distinguishes Mr.
Taylor's interpretation from that of the American revisionists.*

Upsetting traditional or official interpretations of the causes of
a war has long been a favorite occupation of historians on both
sides of the Atlantic, and at times has led to useful reevaluations.
But until this revisionist study appeared in England last spring,
no one seemed to question the fact that the blame for the outbreak of war in 1939 rested firmly and irrefutably upon Hitler.
Hence the excitement over Taylor's pronouncement that it was
as much an outcome of Anglo-French ineptness. Hitler, says
Taylor, neither planned nor wanted war with England and
France.

The Times Literary Supplement, the *Observer,* and the *Guard-
ian* all hailed the brilliance of Taylor's logic, but a fellow Oxford
don, Hugh Trevor-Roper, sternly challenged him with an eight-
thousand-word attack in *Encounter.* "It is not surprising," Trevor-
Roper commented, that Taylor's interpretation "has been hailed
with cries of delight in neo-Nazi or semi-Nazi circles in Germany."

The Origins of the Second World War, augmented, with a
preface addressed to American readers, is now making its appearance in the United States. But it is not likely to be hailed
with delight by those extreme American revisionists who have
ascribed their own country's entrance into the Second World War
to a sinister plot by President Franklin D. Roosevelt, leading to
betrayal at Pearl Harbor. Nor will it please even that handful
who have always felt that if Hitler's western neighbors had left

SOURCE. Frank Freidel "Who Started The War?" *The Reporter,* January 18,
1962.

him to his own devices he would have contented himself with destroying Soviet Russia. At least it will not delight them if they read the book carefully. These American revisionists are a grimly humorless, paranoiac lot, believing intensely in the diabolical foresight and deep-laid conspiracies of their villains. They see everything in sharp blacks and whites, hailing their heroes and hissing their malefactors. They have differed from the rest of the nation partly in the extremes to which they carry their habits of thought, and even more in their choice of demons. For most Americans the man of unsurpassed evil was Hitler.

Taylor's revisionism is of a different sort, a game of endless glittering paradoxes in which he reduces would-be heroes to well-meaning incompetents, and raises popular villains to not far from the same level. From the masses of available evidence, he selects those quotations which serve his thesis, glossing over or discarding those which would mar the brilliant effect. Sparing no one from his witty barbs and destroying no one with righteous wrath, his masterpiece is a startlingly unfamiliar Hitler: a planless opportunist taking advantage of the groping blunderers around him until, undone by his easy successes, he too blunders irretrievably.

This Hitler might seem faintly familiar to those who have read Taylor's earlier books on nineteenth century diplomacy, for Taylor garbs him with patterns of thought and action that might almost be ill-fitting hand-me-downs from Bismarck. Indeed, the whole diplomatic game which Taylor sketches so wryly seems that of the nineteenth century, and the Germans the same people he has previously regarded with such disfavor. In effect, he has recorded the twentieth century cataclysm in neat nineteenth century terms. It is old-fashioned diplomatic history, recounting the maneuvers and countermaneuvers of the antagonists with only an occasional glance at the peoples and issues behind them. It provides the reader with the hypnotic fascination of being a spectator at a chess game, and one loses any sense of observing forces of good and evil. Also as in a chess game, the spectacle that Taylor records has a sort of neatness and inner logic. Stripping the events of the 1930's to the essentials of a diplomatic game does have the advantage of affording new insight, but it creates the equal hazard of new distortion.

The fundamental nature of the game has long been clear to

historians, and in this Taylor presents much the usual views. The conclusion of the First World War, he says, made implicit the outbreak of a second. The German nation, smarting over the Versailles restrictions which humiliated it without rendering it impotent, was marshaled by Hitler to reassert the position as the dominant power in Europe that its population and industrial potential made inevitable. Confronting Germany was a France that wanted security without undue expenditure of economic resources or manpower, and an England ready to accept as morally valid the claims that the Reich should be allowed to expand to incorporate German areas outside its previous borders.

It is in his analysis of the way in which Hitler and his antagonists played the game that Taylor is original. Hitler, he contends, did not operate according to any set plan or timetable, and at no point wished to precipitate a general war. Most of what Hitler said and wrote, even *Mein Kampf,* can be dismissed as empty ranting having little or nothing to do with his actions. The bellicose exhortations to the generals were merely a means to prevent these conservative men from interfering with Hitler's diplomatic moves. "Hitler was a rational, though no doubt a wicked statesman," says Taylor. "His object was the steady extension of German power, not theatrical displays of glory." Operating with an iron nerve, he had merely to make general threats and the English and the French would repeatedly drop in his lap even more than he had demanded. Thus Lord Halifax's remarks when he traveled to Berchtesgaden in November, 1937, "were an invitation to Hitler to promote German nationalist agitation in Danzig, Czechoslovakia, and Austria; an assurance also that this agitation would not be opposed from without."

As long as Hitler was pursuing what the British regarded as morally justifiable goals—consummating the national self-determination of German peoples—those making concessions to him could feel that they were preserving both peace and honor. Even the Munich concessions on the Sudetenland fit under this rubric. Then came the collapse of the rest of Czechoslovakia (which Taylor insists Hitler did not plot or plan), and Britain's attitude sharply changed. Non-Germans were forced into Hitler's new order; that and the general belief that Hitler's word was not to be trusted created a sense of outrage among the British people. Al-

most as an aside, Taylor then mentions what other writers have
with reason elaborated upon at length:

"Of course Hitler's protectorate brought tyranny to Bohemia—
secret police, the S.S., the concentration camps; but no more than
in Germany itself. It was this which roused public opinion in
Great Britain. Hitler's domestic behavior, not his foreign policy,
was the real crime which ultimately brought him—and Germany
—to the ground."

The British and French then promised armed assistance to
Poland, the next potential victim; the Poles stood firm rather
than crumbling as Hitler expected, and out of miscalculations on
both sides over the Danzig crisis came war. Thus runs Taylor's
argument.

In general it is a line of reasoning more notable for its cleverness than its precision. On the Polish crisis it is at its weakest,
since if Hitler really wanted concessions, he could have postponed
his September 1 deadline (arranged the previous April). Taylor
has performed a service in portraying Hitler as a rational man
rather than a maniac, but the reader is likely to underestimate
the viciousness of Hitler's rational program. True, Hitler wanted
to gain all his goals without a major war, but who has ever
doubted this point? A simple gauge of Taylor's book is to com-
pare his pallid, bowdlerized Hitler with Alan Bullock's lifelike
and frightening portrait in *Hitler: A Study in Tyranny* or William L. Shirer's in *The Rise and Fall of the Third Reich*. *The
Origins of the Second World War* is by no means wicked, but
neither is it altogether convincing.

16   *Gordon A. Craig*
Provocative, Perverse View of Pre-1939

Gordon A. Craig, Professor of History at Stanford University, is one of the leading American historians of diplomatic and military history. His works include The Politics of the Prussian Army, 1640–1945 *(Oxford, 1955).*

A. J. P. Taylor's new book is in many ways such a dazzling performance that one almost regrets having to note that its brilliance is exceeded by its perverseness. No one will question the grace and pungency of Mr. Taylor's style, the shrewdness of his insights, or the incisiveness of his comments on such varied figures in the diplomatic world of the interwar years as Stresemann, Briand, Papen, Beck, and Gamelin. The early chapters of this book, which deal with the Versailles settlement and the diplomacy of the 1920's, are masterly; the author's accounts of later episodes, like the tangled Abyssinian affair, are filled with provocative ideas; and his comments on the way in which totalitarian methods of diplomacy tended to demoralize the values and corrupt the policies of democratic statesmen in the 1930's are of striking relevance to our situation policy.

Nevertheless, this is a perverse and potentially dangerous book. Mr. Taylor has always shown a tendency to strain the truth in order to achieve striking formulations. But he has never before been so intent upon demonstrating his originality as he is here, or so willing to indulge in exaggeration, oversimplification, quibbling, and sheer willfulness in order to achieve his effects. He does not even hesitate to make pronouncements that in a soberer mood he would recognize as silly; and, after he has informed us blandly . . . that "the greatest masters of statecraft are those who do not know what they are doing," we have every reason to feel

SOURCE. Gordon A. Craig, "Provocative, Perverse View of Pre-1939," *New York Herald Tribune,* January 7, 1962.

that we have been warned and that we should be suspicious of much that follows.

Mr. Taylor sets out to prove that the Fuehrer never had any long-range foreign policy plans at all and that he most certainly never wanted war, which came upon him, when it came, largely by accident. Hitler, he intimates, has never been properly understood, and the idea has got around that he was an evil man. On the contrary, "in principle and doctrine, he was no more wicked and unscrupulous than many other contemporary statesmen," although Mr. Taylor adds almost as an after-thought—"in wicked acts he outdid them all."

Leaving the question of Hitler's wickedness aside (and one can never be quite sure whether the principles of the act are more important in Mr. Taylor's mind), the Fuehrer certainly had more precise views on foreign policy than one would gather from this book. Indeed, one of the impressive things about Hitler is the consistency of his thinking on foreign affairs from the days when he was a beer-hall orator in the 1920s until he was in a position to give his ideas substance. Mr. Taylor can deny this only by ignoring the clear evidence of its truth or attempting to explain it away and he does both. For one thing, as H. R. Trevor-Roper pointed out in his magisterial review of the English edition of this book, he denies that *Mein Kampf*, the book in which Hitler sketched the main lines of his future policy in 1924, had any importance whatsoever. For another, he refuses to accept any later utterances of Hitler as evidence of systematic thinking about foreign policy. Thus, he denies the significance of Hitler's declaration to his military commanders on 5 November 1937. This has been generally accepted as an important reformulation of the Fuehrer's policy views and a sign of their early implementation. Mr. Taylor believes that Hitler's remarks on this occasion show no evidence of systematic thinking, let alone aggressive intent, and he adds that "they bear hardly any relation to the actual outbreak of war in 1939."

Yet at the meeting in question Hitler declared that he wanted "to explain to the gentlemen present his basic ideas concerning the opportunities for the development of our position in the field of foreign affairs and its requirements, and he asked, in the interests of a long-term German policy, that his exposition be

regarded, in the event of his death, as his last will and testament."
He then proceeded to elaborate on the idea, first laid down in
Mein Kampf, that Germany's security depended on the acquisi-
tion of a great empire in eastern Europe, and added that this
"problem could only be solved by means of force and this was
never without attendant risk." When the time to use force
arrived, Germany must "overthrow" Czechoslovakia and Austria
simultaneously in order to remove the threat to our flank in any
possible operation against the West." This surely should be systematic enough even for Mr. Taylor. Moreover, since both Austria
and Czechoslovakia *were* attacked before another year had passed,
and since this facilitated the attack on Poland which in turn led
to the attack on the West, Mr. Taylor's denial of the relevance of
Hitler's remarks to the outbreak of war is preposterous.

Mr. Taylor is so eager to upset accepted views that he comes
close to absolving Hitler from responsibility for anything that
happened after 1933. That the Fuehrer began to move against
eastern Europe in 1938 was largely the result, he intimates, of
suggestions made to him by Chamberlain and Halifax. The fall
of Austria was thus due to the delinquencies of others, and the
rape of Czechoslovakia "was not of his making" either. "Geography and politics automatically put Czechoslovakia on the
agenda;" and, in any case, the Czechs invited their own destruction by having a nationalities problem. As for Poland, she "signed
her death-warrant" on 30 March 1939 when she accepted Britain's
pledge of assistance in case of aggression, for it was Colonel
Beck's insistence on the letter of this agreement that made any
peaceful solution impossible.

In making his case, Mr. Taylor is not worried by inconsistencies and contradictions. The idea that "Hitler's seizure of Austria
was a deliberate plot, devised long in advance [is] a myth," he
says. "The crisis of March 1938 was provoked by Schuschnigg,
not by Hitler." Two sentences later, he admits that Hitler had for
a long time "certainly meant to establish control over Austria;"
but, he adds, "the way in which this came about was for him a
tiresome accident, an interruption of his long-term policy." Why
it was tiresome he does not explain; nor does he remember that
a few pages earlier he was arguing that Hitler had no long-term
policy.

Another example of the same sort of thing is his treatment of the question whether Hitler wanted war in 1939. "Many . . . believe that Hitler was a modern Attila, loving destruction for its own sake and therefore bent on war without thought of policy. There is no arguing with such dogmas . . . [In reality] he was intending to succeed without war, or at any rate only with a war so nominal as hardly to be distinguished from diplomacy." The qualification makes nonsense of the argument. Hitler may have thought that Britain and France would not go to war for Poland, but that he himself desired war with Poland is beyond doubt. Ribbentrop admitted this brutally to Ciano in August 1939 and, in a speech to his generals in the same month, Hitler did the same, adding that he was "only afraid that some Schweinehund will make a proposal of mediation." To say that he was "probably not intending war at all" is belied by the facts; and Hitler's stubborn insistence about attacking Poland brought on the greater conflict.

Of one of his own theories, Mr. Taylor says "this is . . . worth developing, if only as an academic exercise." One suspects that there are too many such exercises in this book. The most remarkable is the author's demonstration that Munich was "not a triumph for Hitler" but (since it rectified a situation in which a German minority lived under Czech government) "a triumph for all that was best and most enlightened in British life; a triumph for those who had preached equal justice between peoples; a triumph for those who had courageously denounced the harshness and shortsightedness of Versailles." This makes the imagination boggle; and anyone who remembers that Munich prepared the way for the death of central Europe's only remaining democracy will reject Mr. Taylor's sophistication in favor of the brutal common sense of that nameless British M. P. who, upon being informed of the contents of the Munich Treaty, said, "If that's all Neville could get, why did he go to Munich? He could have written that on the back of a dirty postcard and sent it home from Brighton."

In the introduction to this American edition, Mr. Taylor complains that English reviewers have accused him of writing an apologia for Hitler, and he says that this was not his intention. This may well be. But an historian who can, without any qualification whatsoever, describe Chamberlain, Halifax, Daladier, and Bonnet as "the four men who, between them, settled the destinies of Western civilization" lays himself open to the charge of minimizing Hitler's responsibility for the coming of war in 1939. He also gives aid and comfort to those who would like to rehabilitate the Fuehrer's reputation.

17   *Raymond J. Sontag*
        The Origins of the Second World War

Professor Raymond J. Sontag of the University of California at Berkeley is a distinguished scholar of German history. He is the author of Germany and England, Background of Conflict, 1848– 1898 *(New York, 1938), and an editor of the series of German Foreign Office documents.*

A. J. P. Taylor presents the thesis that the responsibility for the coming of the Second World War rests not at all on the Soviet Union, very little on Hitler, and very much on Britain, with France as a reluctant accomplice. Since the thesis, as he repeatedly points out, runs counter to the prevailing scholarly interpretation of the evidence, the reader has a right to expect care and precision in the handling of the evidence.

The reader will find neither. Two sentences on a single page may serve as illustrations, both relating to the meeting of Hitler with Mussolini in 1934. The first deals with the preparations for the meeting. "He [Hitler] said in the Council of Ministers: 'I am ready to write off Austria for years to come, but I cannot say so

SOURCE. Raymond J. Sontag, in the *American Historical Review*, July 1962, Vol. 67, No. 4, pp. 992–994. Reprinted by permission of the American Historical Association and the author.

to Mussolini.' " The reference given by Taylor is to a memorandum by Bülow printed in *Documents on German Foreign Policy*, Series C, Volume II, Number 393. At the outet, Bülow listed the participants in the conference: Hitler, the Foreign Minister, the *Reichswehr* Minister, the ambassador in Italy, and Bülow. This was not "the Council of Ministers." As for the supposed direct quotation of Hitler's words, what Bülow actually wrote was very different: "He [Hitler] was quite ready to write Austria off for years to come and hand her over to economic fertilization by Italy; this in any case could not get very far and was basically only a hopeless attempt to revive the ports of Trieste and Fiume. But he was not willing to give the Italian Chief of Government such a statement of disinterestedness in precise wording, not to mention in writing."

Taylor's second sentence deals with the meeting of Hitler and Mussolini: "Hitler renounced, truthfully enough, any desire to annex Austria." In support of his account of the meeting, Taylor refers the reader to two documents in the series cited above. In neither of these does Hitler renounce "any desire to annex Austria." In the first, he was reported to have said: "The question of the *Anschluss* was of no interest since it was in no way acute and, as he was well aware, internally not feasible." In the second, the Italian summary, he was reported to have said: "The *Anschluss* is not an immediate aim of Germany's policy."

These inaccuracies, taken by themselves, may seem only regrettable carelessness. But they, and others, form the basis upon which is built an important generalization: "He [Hitler] was Austrian enough to find the complete disappearance of Austria inconceivable until it happened; even if conceivable, it was unwelcome to him that Vienna (to say nothing of Linz) should be eclipsed by Berlin." As anyone acquainted with the evidence knows, acceptance of this generalization requires the elimination of a formidable body of evidence, beginning with *Mein Kampf*, the opening sentences of which call for the "return" of Austria to "the great German motherland." Those opening sentences, and much that follows, make a mockery of Taylor's larger generalization, that Hitler was interested in power, not territory, and therefore that his territorial acquisitions of 1938–1939, beginning with Austria and ending with Poland, resulted in large part from the ill-advised maneuvers of Schuschnigg, or Beneš, or Hacha, or Beck, and not from his own aggressive designs. Taylor therefore takes great pains to discredit *Mein Kampf* and those who have used *Mein Kampf* as an aid to the understanding of German policy. His approach may be illustrated by a sentence dealing with the great shift of British opinion after March 15, 1939: "Others attributed to him [Hitler] new and more grandiose plans which they claimed to have discovered by reading *Mein Kampf* in the original (Hitler forbade its publication in English)." Actually, of course, such grandiose plans are to be found in *Mein Kampf*, and actually Englishmen were not dependent on what those who had read the original claimed they had discovered; a detailed review of the unexpurgated English translation appeared in the *Times Literary Supplement* for March 25, 1939. Parenthetically, to foreclose the claim that, in the sentence quoted, Taylor did not say *Mein Kampf* had not been translated, the index contains the notation "*Mein Kampf* .... not translated into English, 204."

In the examples given above, it has been possible to demonstrate briefly the manipulation of the evidence. Such demonstration, for the larger and more complex issues, is impossible within the compass of a review. Let me conclude with one illustration of Taylor's method which does touch the central issue. For him, Munich "was a triumph for all that was best and most enlightened in British life" because British policy "originated in the belief that Germany had a moral right to the Sudeten German territory, on grounds of national principle." On the other hand, he professes inability to understand the shift of British opinion after March 15, 1939. "The occupation of Prague," he maintains, "did not represent anything new in Hitler's policy or behavior." He offers many possible explanations for the shift in British opinion, but he never mentions the one obvious explanation: that, while the annexation of Austria and the Sudeten German territory could be justified on the ground of self-determination, the annexation of the Czech territory showed that Hitler had taken the path of conquest.

With the demand for Danzig, Taylor resumes the theme of self-determination, and from that point treats British policy as foolish, blindly foolish, while the drawing together of Germany and Russia is made to seem only a desperate effort to avoid the tragedy of war toward which British policy was dragging Europe.

18   *Alan Bullock*
Hitler and the Origins of the Second World War

Alan Bullock is the Master of St. Catherine's College, Oxford.
His biography of Hitler is generally regarded as the best work on
the subject.

I

In the twenty years since the end of the war and the Nuremberg Trials, historical controversy has been largely concerned
with the share of the other Powers in the responsibility for allowing war to break out in 1939. Thus, the British and French
Governments of the 1930s have been blamed for their policy of
appeasement and for failing to secure an agreement with Russia;
Mussolini for his alliance with Hitler; Stalin for the Nazi-Soviet
Pact; the Poles for the illusions which encouraged them to believe that they could hold Russia as well as Germany at arm's
length. Taking a wider sweep, historians have turned for an explanation of the origins of the Second World War to the mistakes
made in the peace settlement that followed the First; to the in-
adequacies of British and French policy between the wars; the
retreat of the United States into isolation; the exclusion of the
Soviet Union; the social effects of the Great Depression, and so
on.

All this is necessary work, in order to establish the historical
situation in which the war began, but as the catalogue grows, I
find myself asking what is left of the belief universally held outside Germany twenty years ago that the primary responsibility
for the war rested on Hitler and the Nazis?

No one suggests that theirs was the sole responsibility. Hitler
would never have got as near to success as he did if it had not
been for the weakness, the divisions, the opportunism of the other

SOURCE. Alan Bullock, "Hitler and the Origins of the Second World War,"
Proceedings of the British Academy, LIII (1967). Reprinted by permission of
The British Academy.

governments, which allowed him to build up such power that he could not be prevented from conquering Europe without a major war. Still, there is a lot of difference between failing to stop aggression, even hoping to derive side profits from it—and aggression itself. Indeed, much of the criticism directed at the other Powers for their failure to stop Hitler in time would fall to the ground if there proved to have been nothing to stop.

Is the effect of filling in the historical picture to reduce this difference to the point where it no longer appears so important, where the responsibility for the war becomes dispersed, or is shifted on to the shortcomings of an anarchical system of international relations, or of militarism or of capitalism, as happened after the First World War? Is Mr. A. J. P. Taylor the harbinger of a new generation of revisionist historians who will find it as anachronistic to hold Hitler—or anyone else—responsible for the outbreak of the Second World War as to hold the Kaiser responsible for the outbreak of the First?

The question is an important one, for to an extent which we only begin to realize when it is questioned, the accepted version of European history in the years between 1933 and 1945 has been built round a particular view of Hitler and of the character of German foreign policy, and if the centrepiece were removed, far more than our view of Hitler and German foreign policy would have to be revised—our view of the foreign policies of all the Powers and of the substantiality of the dangers which the other governments, and their critics, believed they confronted.

It occurred to me, therefore, when I was invited to deliver this lecture, that it would be interesting to take a fresh look at Hitler's foreign policy in the light of the new evidence that has become available in the twenty years since the Nuremberg Trials (and, no less important, of new ways of looking at familiar evidence) and then to go on and ask, in what sense, if at all, it is still possible to speak of Hitler's and the Nazis' responsibility for what became a Second World War.

II

There are two contrasted versions of Hitler's foreign policy which for convenience's sake I will call the fanatic and the opportunist.

The first fastens upon Hitler's racist views and his insistence that the future of the German people could be secured, neither by economic development nor by overseas colonization, not even by the restoration of Germany's 1914 frontiers, but only by the conquest of living space (*Lebensraum*) in Eastern Europe. Here the scattered populations of Germans living outside the Reich could be concentrated, together with the surplus population of the homeland, and a Germanic empire established, racially homogeneous, economically self-sufficient, and militarily impregnable. Such *Lebensraum* could only be obtained at the expense of Russia and the states bordering on her and could only be won and cleared of its existing population by force, a view which coincided with Hitler's belief in struggle as the law of life, and war as the test of a people's racial superiority.

Hitler first set these views down in *Mein Kampf*, elaborated them in his so-called *Zweites Buch*, and repeated them on almost every occasion when we have a record of him talking privately and not in public, down to the Table Talk of the 1940s and his final conversations with Bormann in the early months of 1945 when his defeat could no longer be disguised. Not only did he consistently hold and express these views over twenty years, but in 1941 he set to work to put them into practice in the most literal way, by attacking Russia and by giving full rein to his plans, which the S.S. had already begun to carry out in Poland, for the resettlement of huge areas of Eastern Europe.

The alternative version treats Hitler's talk of *Lebensraum* and racist empire in the East as an expression of the fantasy side of his personality and fastens on the opportunism of Hitler's actual conduct of foreign policy. In practice—so this version runs— Hitler was an astute and cynical politician who took advantage of the mistakes and illusions of others to extend German power along lines entirely familiar from the previous century of German history. So little did he take his own professions seriously that he actually concluded a pact with the Bolsheviks whom he had denounced, and when Hitler belatedly began to put his so-called programme into practice, it marked the point at which he lost the capacity to distinguish between fantasy and reality and, with it, the opportunist's touch which had been responsible for his long run of successes. Thereafter he suffered nothing but one disaster after another.

These two versions of Hitler's foreign policy correspond to

alternative versions of his personality. The first stresses his insis
tence on a fanatical will, force, and brutality of purpose, his conviction that he was a man of destiny, his reliance on intuition,
his scorn for compromise, his declaration after the occupation of
the Rhineland: "I go the way that Providence dictates with the
assurance of a sleepwalker."

The second takes this no more seriously than the rest of Nazi
and Fascist rhetoric and insists that in practice Hitler relied for
his success upon calculation, total lack of scruple, and remarkable
gifts as an actor. The suggestion that his opponents had to deal
with a man who was fanatical in his purposes and would stop at
nothing to accomplish them was part of the act, and a very successful part. His threats were carefully timed as part of a war of
nerves, his ungovernable rages turned on or off as the occasion
demanded, his hypnotic stare and loss of control part of a public
persona skilfully and cynically manipulated. And when Hitler,
carried away by his triumphs, himself began to believe in his own
myth, and no longer to manipulate it, success deserted him.

It is a mistake, however, I believe, to treat these two contrasting
views as alternatives, for if that is done, then, whichever alternative is adopted, a great deal of evidence has to be ignored. The
truth is, I submit, that they have to be combined and that Hitler
can only be understood if it is realized that he was at once both
fanatical *and* cynical; unyielding in his assertion of will-power
and cunning in calculation; convinced of his role as a man of
destiny *and* prepared to use all the actor's arts in playing it. To
leave out either side, the irrational or the calculating, is to fail to
grasp the combination which marks Hitler out from all his imita-
tors.

The same argument, I believe, applies to Hitler's foreign policy
which combined consistency of aim with complete opportunism
in method and tactics. This is, after all, a classical receipt for
success in foreign affairs. It was precisely because he knew where
he wanted to go that Hitler could afford to be opportunistic and
saw how to take advantage of the mistakes and fears of others.
Consistency of aim on Hitler's part has been confused with a
time-table, blueprint, or plan of action fixed in advance, as if it
were pinned up on the wall of the General Staff offices and ticked
off as one item succeeded another. Nothing of the sort. Hitler

frequently improvised, kept his options open to the last possible moment, and was never sure until he got there which of several courses of action he would choose. But this does not alter the fact that his moves followed a logical (though not a predetermined) course—in contrast to Mussolini, an opportunist who snatched eagerly at any chance that was going but never succeeded in combining even his successes into a coherent policy.

III

Hitler had established his power inside Germany by the late summer of 1934. By securing the succession to President Hindenburg, he became Head of State and Commander-in-Chief of the Armed Forces as well as leader of the only party in the country and head of a government in which no one dared to oppose him. From now on, apart from the one thing which he put before everything else, his own supremacy, Hitler took no great interest in internal affairs or administration. He turned his attention almost wholly to foreign policy and rearmament.

Shortly after he became Chancellor, on 3 February 1933, Hitler had met the leaders of the armed forces privately and told them that, once his political power was secure, his most important task would be to rearm Germany and then move from the revision of the Versailles Treaty to the conquest of *Lebensraum* in the East.

Just over a year later, on 28 February 1934, Hitler repeated this at a conference of Army and S.A. leaders, declaring that here was a decisive reason for rejecting Roehm's plan for a national militia and for rebuilding the German Army. The Western Powers would never allow Germany to conquer *Lebensraum* in the East. "Therefore, short decisive blows to the West and then to the East could be necessary," tasks which could only be carried out by an army rigorously trained and equipped with the most modern weapons.

None the less, in the first two years, 1933 and 1934, Hitler's foreign policy was cautious. Politically, he had still to establish his own supremacy at home. Diplomatically, Germany was isolated and watched with suspicion by all her neighbours. Militarily, she was weak and unable to offer much resistance if the French or the Poles should take preventive action against the new régime.

These were all excellent reasons for Hitler to protest his love of

peace and innocence of aggressive intentions. As he told Rau
schning, now that Germany had left Geneva, he would more than
ever speak "the language of the League." There is, in fact, a
striking parallel between his conduct of foreign policy in this
early period and the tactics of "legality" which he had pursued
in his struggle for power inside Germany. By observing the forms
of legality, staying within the framework of the constitution, and
refusing to make a *Putsch*—which would have brought the Nazis
into open conflict with the Army—Hitler was able to turn the
weapons of democracy against democracy itself. His appeal to
Wilsonian principles of national self-determination and equality
of rights had precisely the same effect—and those who believed
him were to be as sharply disillusioned as those who supposed
Hitler would continue to observe the limits of legality in Germany once he had acquired the power to ignore them.

Although Nazi propaganda made the most of them, none of
Hitler's foreign policy moves in his first two years did much to
improve Germany's position. Leaving the Disarmament Conference and the League was a gesture; the Pact with Poland clever
but unconvincing, and more than counter-balanced by Russia's
agreement to join the League and start negotiations for an alliance with France. The hurried repudiation of the Austrian Nazis
in 1934 was humiliating, and the Saar plebiscite in January 1935
was largely a foregone conclusion. When Hitler announced the
reintroduction of conscription in March 1935, Germany's action
was condemned by the British, French, and Italian governments
meeting at Stresa, as well as by the League Council, and was
answered by the conclusion of pacts between Russia and France,
and Russia and France's most reliable ally Czechoslovakia.

Between 1935 and 1937, however, the situation changed to
Hitler's advantage, and he was able not only to remove the limitations of the Versailles Treaty on Germany's freedom of action but
to break out of Germany's diplomatic isolation.

It is true that the opportunities for this were provided by the
other Powers: for example, by Mussolini's Abyssinian adventure
and the quarrel to which this led between Italy and the Western
Powers. But Hitler showed skill in using the opportunities which
others provided, for example, in Spain where he reduced the
policy of non-intervention to a farce and exploited the civil war

for his own purposes with only a minimum commitment to Franco. He also provided his own opportunities: for example, the offer of a naval treaty to Britain in 1935 and the military reoccupation of the Rhineland in 1930. This was a bold and risky stroke of bluff, taken against the advice of his generals, without anything like sufficient forces to resist the French if they had marched, and accompanied by a brilliantly contrived diversion in the form of the new peace pacts which he offered simultaneously to the other Locarno Powers.

Of course, there were failures—above all, Ribbentrop's failure to get an alliance with Britain. But between April 1935, when the Powers, meeting at Stresa, had unanimously condemned German rearmament, and Mussolini's state visit to Germany as a prospective ally in September 1937, Hitler could claim with some justification to have transformed Germany's diplomatic position and ended her isolation.

IV

The German Foreign Ministry and diplomatic service were well suited to the international equivalent of the policy of "legality," but Hitler soon began to develop instruments of his own for a new style of foreign policy. One was the Nazi groups among the Volksdeutsche living abroad. The two most obvious examples are the Nazi Party in Austria and Henlein's *Sudetendeutsche Partei* in Czechoslovakia. The former had to be hastily disavowed in the summer of 1934, when the *Putsch* against Dolfuss failed, but the subsidies to the Austrian Nazis continued and so did the many links across the frontier from Munich and Berlin. Henlein's Sudeten Party was also secretly in receipt of subsidies from Germany from early 1935, and was to play a key role in the campaign against Czechoslovakia. These links were maintained outside the regular Foreign Ministry system and there were a number of Nazi agencies—Bohle's *Auslandsorganisation*, Rosenberg's *Aussenpolitisches Amt*, VOMI (*Volksdeutsche Mittelstelle*) competing with each other, and with the Foreign Ministry, to organize the German-speaking groups living abroad.

At the same time Hitler began to make use of envoys from outside the foreign service for the most important diplomatic negotiations: Goering, for instance, who frequently undertook special missions to Italy, Poland, and the Balkans, and Ribbentrop whose Büro, originally set up to deal with disarmament questions in 1933, soon moved into direct competition with the *Auswärtiges Amt*. It was Ribbentrop who negotiated the naval treaty with London; Ribbentrop who was given the key post of ambassador in London in order to secure a British alliance; Ribbentrop who represented Germany on the Non-Intervention Committee, who negotiated and signed the Anti-Comintern Pact with Japan in 1936 and a year later brought in Italy as well.

It was not until the beginning of 1938 that Hitler appointed Ribbentrop as Foreign Minister: until then he left the German Foreign Ministry and diplomatic service as a respectable façade but increasingly took the discussion of policy and the decisions out of their hands and used other agents to carry them out. In Hitler's eyes the diplomats—like the generals, as he came to feel during the war—were too conservative, too preoccupied with the conventional rules of the game to see the advantages of scrapping rules altogether and taking opponents by surprise. Hitler's radicalism required a new style in the conduct of foreign affairs as different from old style diplomacy as the Nazi Party was from the old style political parties of the Weimar Republic.

This new style did not emerge clearly until 1938–9, but there were unmistakable signs of it before then in the changed tone in which Hitler and German propaganda were speaking by 1937. Hitler receiving Mussolini and showing off the strength of the new Germany, Hitler beginning to talk of Germany's "demands," was speaking a very different language from that of the man who only three or four years before had used all his gifts as an orator to convince the world of Germany's will to peace. German national pride and self-confidence had been restored, and, instead of trying to conceal, Nazi propaganda now boasted of her growing military strength.

V

The Nazis' claims about German rearmament were widely believed. Phrases like "Guns before butter"—"total war"—"a war economy in peacetime" made a deep impression. When Goering was appointed Plenipotentiary for the Four Year Plan in October 1936, this was taken to mean the speeding up of rearmament, and

Hitler's secret memorandum to Goering found among Speer's papers after the war confirms this view. Irritated by Schacht's opposition to his demands, he declared that the shortage of raw-materials was "not an economic problem, but solely a question of will." A clash with Bolshevik Russia was unavoidable: "No State will be able to withdraw or even remain at a distance from this historical conflict. . . . We cannot escape this destiny."

Hitler concluded his memorandum to Goering with the words:

"I thus set the following task:

1. The German Army must be operational (*einsatzfähig*) within 4 years.

2. The German economy must be fit for war (*kriegsfähig*) within 4 years."

Yet the evidence now available does not bear out the widespread belief in Germany's all-out rearmament before 1939. The figures show that the rearmament programme took a long time to get under way and did not really begin to produce the results Hitler wanted until 1939. Even then Germany's military superiority was not as great as both public opinion and the Allies' intelligence services assumed.

The really surprising fact, however, is the scale of German rearmament in relation to Germany's economic resources. At no time before September 1939 was anything like the full capacity of the German economy devoted to war production. The figures are well below what German industry could have achieved if fully mobilized, below what German industry had achieved in 1914–18, and below what was achieved by the British when they set about rearmament in earnest.

The immediate conclusion which one might well draw from these facts is that they provide powerful support for the argument that Hitler was not deliberately preparing for war but was thinking in terms of an armed diplomacy in which he relied on bluff and the *threat* of war to blackmail or frighten the other Powers into giving way to his demands.

Before we accept this conclusion, however, it is worth while to carry the examination of the rearmament figures beyond the date of 1 September 1939. The attack on Poland may or may not have been due to mistaken calculation on Hitler's part (I shall come back to this later), but no one can doubt that the German attack on France and the Low Countries on 10 May 1940 was deliberate, not hastily improvised but prepared for over a six months' period. And this time it was an attack not on a second-class power like Poland but on two major Powers, France and Britain. Yet the interesting fact is that the proportion of Germany's economic resources devoted to the war hardly went up at all. Even more striking, the same is true of the attack on Russia in 1941. In preparation for Operation Barbarossa, the Army was built up to 180 divisions, but this was not accompanied by an all-out armaments drive and on the very eve of the invasion of Russia (20 June 1941) Hitler actually ordered a reduction in the level of arms production. This was put into effect and by December 1941, when the German Army was halted before Moscow, the over-all level of weapons production had fallen by 29 per cent. from its peak in July of that year.

In fact, it was not until 1942, the year in which Hitler lost the initiative and Germany was pushed on to the defensive, that Hitler was persuaded to commit the full resources of the German economy to an all-out effort.

This puts the facts I have mentioned in a different light. For, if Hitler believed that he could defeat the Western Powers, subdue the Balkans, and conquer Russia without demanding more than a partial mobilization from the German people, then the fact that German rearmament before the war had limited rather than total objectives is no proof that his plans at that time did not include war.

The truth is that, both before and after September 1939, Hitler was thinking in terms of a very different sort of war from that which Germany had lost in 1914–18 or was to lose again between 1942 and 1945. With a shrewder judgement than many of his military critics, Hitler realized that Germany, with limited resources of her own and subject to a blockade, was always going to be at a disadvantage in a long-drawn-out general war. The sort of war she could win was a series of short campaigns in which surprise and the overwhelming force of the initial blow would settle the issue before the victim had time to mobilize his full resources or the other Powers to intervene. This was the sort of war the German Army was trained as well as equipped to fight, and all the German campaigns between 1939 and 1941 conformed to this pattern—Poland, four weeks; Norway, two months; Holland, five days, Belgium, seventeen; France, six weeks; Yugoslavia, eleven days; Greece, three weeks. The most interesting case of all is that of Russia. The explanation of why the German Army was allowed to invade Russia without winter clothing or equipment is Hitler's belief that even Russia could be knocked out by a blitzkrieg in four to five months, before the winter set in. And so convinced was Hitler that he had actually achieved this that in his directive of 14 July 1941 he spoke confidently of reducing the size of the Army, the Navy, and the armaments programme in the near future.

This pattern of warfare, very well adapted both to Germany's economic position and the advantages of secrecy and surprise enjoyed by a dictatorship, fits perfectly the pattern of German rearmament. What was required was not armament in depth, the long-term conversion of the whole economy to a war footing which (as in Britain) would only begin to produce results in two to three years, but a war economy of a different sort geared (like German strategy) to the concept of the blitzkrieg. It was an economy which concentrated on a short-term superiority and the weapons which could give a quick victory, even when this meant neglecting the proper balance of a long-term armament programme. What mattered, as Hitler said in his 1936 memorandum, was not stocks of raw materials or building up productive capacity, but armaments ready for use, plus the will to use them. How near the gamble came to success is shown by the history of the years 1939–41 when Hitler's limited rearmament programme produced an army capable of overrunning the greater part of Europe, and very nearly defeating the Russians as well as the French.

VI

But we must not run ahead of the argument. The fact that Germany was better prepared for war, and when it began proceeded to win a remarkable series of victories, does not prove that Hitler intended to start the war which actually broke out in September 1939. We have still to relate Hitler's long-term plans for expansion in the East and his rearmament programme to the actual course of events in 1938 and 1939.

A starting-point is Colonel Hossbach's record of Hitler's conference with his three Commanders-in-Chief, War Minister, and Foreign Minister on 5 November 1937. It was an unusual occasion, since Hitler rarely talked to more than one Commander-in-Chief or minister at a time, and he came nearer to laying down a programme than he ever had before. Once again he named *Lebensraum* in the East and the need to provide for Germany's future by continental expansion as the objective, but instead of leaving it at that, he went on to discuss how this was to be achieved.

The obstacles in the way were Britain and France, Germany's two "hate-inspired antagonists." Neither was as strong as she seemed: still, "Germany's problems could only be solved by force and this was never without attendant risk."

The peak of German power would be reached in 1943–5: after that, their·lead in armaments would be reduced. "It was while the rest of the world was preparing its defences that we were obliged to take the offensive." Whatever happened, he was resolved to solve Germany's problem of space by 1943–5 at the latest. Hitler then discussed two possible cases in which action might be taken earlier—one was civil strife in France, disabling the French Army: the other, war in the Mediterranean which might allow Germany to act as early as 1938. The first objective in either case "must be to overthrow Czechoslovakia and Austria simultaneously in order to remove the threat to our flank in any possible operation against the West." Hitler added the comment that almost certainly Britain and probably France as well had already tacitly written off the Czechs.

To speak of this November meeting as a turning-point in Hitler's foreign policy at which Hitler made an irreversible decision in favour of war seems to me as wide of the target as talking about time-tables and blueprints of aggression. Hitler was far too skilful a politician to make irreversible decisions in advance of events: no decisions were taken or called for.

But to brush the Hossbach meeting aside and say that this was just Hitler talking for effect and not to be taken seriously seems to me equally wide of the mark. The hypotheses Hitler outlined —civil strife in France, a Mediterranean war—did not materialize, but when Hitler spoke of his determination to overthrow Czechoslovakia and Austria, as early as 1938 if an opportunity offered, and when both countries *were* overthrown within less than eighteen months, it is stretching incredulity rather far to ignore the fact that he had stated this as his immediate programme in November 1937.

The next stage was left open, but Hitler foresaw quite correctly that everything would depend upon the extent to which Britain and France were prepared to intervene by force to prevent Germany's continental expansion and he clearly contemplated war if they did. Only when the obstacle which they represented had been removed would it be possible for Germany to carry out her eastward expansion.

This was a better forecast of the direction of events in 1938–41 than any other European leader including Stalin made at the end of 1937—for the very good reason that Hitler, however opportunist in his tactics, knew where he wanted to go, was almost alone among European leaders in knowing this, and so kept the initiative in his hands.

The importance of the Hossbach conference, I repeat, is not in recording a decision, but in reflecting the change in Hitler's attitude. If the interpretation offered of his policy in 1933–7 is correct, it was not a sudden but a gradual change, and a change not in the objectives of foreign policy but in Hitler's estimate of the risks he could afford to take in moving more rapidly and openly towards them. As he told the Nazi Old Guard at Augsburg a fortnight later: "I am convinced that the most difficult part of the preparatory work has already been achieved. . . . Today we are faced with new tasks, for the *Lebensraum* of our people is too narrow."

There is another point to be made about the Hossbach conference. Of the five men present besides Hitler and his adjutant Hossbach, Goering was certainly not surprised by what he heard and Raeder said nothing. But the other three, the two generals and Neurath, the Foreign Minister, showed some alarm and expressed doubts. It is surely another remarkable coincidence if this had nothing to do with the fact that within three months all three men had been turned out of office—the two generals, Blomberg and Fritsch, on bare-faced pretexts. There is no need to suppose that Hitler himself took the initiative in framing Blomberg or Fritsch. The initiative seems more likely to have come from Goering and Himmler, but it was Hitler who turned both Blomberg's *mésalliance* and the allegations against Fritsch to his own political advantage. Blomberg, the Minister of War, was replaced by Hitler himself who suppressed the office altogether, took over the OKW, the High Command of the armed forces, as his own staff and very soon made clear that neither the OKW nor the OKH, the High Command of the Army, would be allowed the independent position of the old General Staff. Fritsch, long regarded by Hitler as too stiff, conservative, and out of sympathy with Nazi ideas, was replaced by the much more pliable Brauchitsch as Commander-in-Chief of the Army, and Neurath, a survivor from the original coalition, by Ribbentrop who made it as clear to the staff of the Foreign Ministry as Hitler did to the generals that they were there to carry out orders, not to discuss, still less question the Fuehrer's policy.

VII

I find nothing at all inconsistent with what I have just said in the fact that the timing for the first of Hitler's moves, the annexation of Austria, should have been fortuitous and the preparations for it improvised on the spur of the moment in a matter of days, almost of hours. On the contrary, the *Anschluss* seems to me to provide, almost in caricature, a striking example of that extraordinary combination of consistency in aim, calculation, and patience in preparation with opportunism, impulse, and improvisation in execution which I regard as characteristic of Hitler's policy.

The aim in this case was never in doubt: the demand for the incorporation of Austria in the Reich appears on the first page of *Mein Kampf*. After the Austrian Nazis' unsuccessful *Putsch* of 1934, Hitler showed both patience and skill in his relations with Austria: he gradually disengaged Mussolini from his commitment to maintain Austrian independence and at the same time steadily undermined that independence from within. By the beginning of 1938 he was ready to put on the pressure, but the invitation to Schuschnigg to come to Berchtesgaden was made on the spur of the moment as the result of a suggestion by an anxious Papen trying hard to find some pretext to defer his own recall from Vienna. When Schuschnigg appeared on 12 February, Hitler put on an elaborate act to frighten him into maximum concessions with the threat of invasion, but there is no reason to believe that either Hitler or the generals he summoned to act as "stage extras" regarded these threats as anything other than bluff. Hitler was confident that he would secure Austria, without moving a man, simply by the appointment of his nominee Seyss-Inquart as Minister of the Interior and the legalization of the Austrian Nazis —to both of which Schuschnigg agreed.

When the Austrian Chancellor, in desperation, announced a plebiscite on 9 March, Hitler was taken completely by surprise. Furious at being crossed, he decided at once to intervene before the plebiscite could be held. But no plans for action had been prepared: they had to be improvised in the course of a single day, and everything done in such a hurry and confusion that 70 per cent of the tanks and lorries, according to General Jodl, broke down on the road to Vienna. The confusion was even greater in the Reich Chancellery: when Schuschnigg called off the plebiscite, Hitler hesitated, then was persuaded by Goering to let the march in continue, but without any clear idea of what was to follow. Only when he reached Linz, did Hitler, by then in a state of self-intoxication, suddenly decide to annex Austria instead of making it a satellite state, and his effusive messages of relief to Mussolini show how unsure he was of the consequences of his action.

No doubt the *Anschluss* is an exceptional case. On later occasions the plans were ready: dates by which both the Czech and the Polish crises must be brought to a solution were fixed well in advance, and nothing like the same degree of improvisation was necessary. But in all the major crises of Hitler's career there is the same strong impression of confusion at the top, springing directly (as his generals and aides complained) from his own hesitations and indecision. It is to be found in his handling of domestic as well as foreign crises—as witness his long hesitation before the Roehm purge of 1934—and in war as well as peacetime.

The paradox is that out of all this confusion and hesitation there should emerge a series of remarkably bold decisions, just as, out of Hitler's opportunism in action, there emerges a pattern which conforms to objectives stated years before.

VIII

The next crisis, directed against Czechoslovakia, was more deliberately staged. This time Hitler gave preliminary instructions to his staff on 21 April 1938 and issued a revised directive on 30 May. Its first sentence read: "It is my unalterable decision to smash Czechoslovakia by military action in the near future." It was essential, Hitler declared, to create a situation within the first two or three days which would make intervention by other Powers hopeless: the Army and the Air Force were to concentrate all their strength for a knock-out blow and leave only minimum forces to hold Germany's other frontiers.

It is perfectly true that for a long time in the summer Hitler kept out of the way and left the other Powers to make the running, but this was only part of the game. Through Henlein and the Sudeten Party, who played the same role of fifth column as the Austrian Nazis, Hitler was able to manipulate the dispute between the Sudeten Germans and the Czech Government, which was the ostensible cause of the crisis, from within. At a secret meeting with Hitler on 28 March, Henlein summarized his policy in the words: "We must always demand so much that we can never be satisfied." The Fuehrer, says the official minute, approved this view.

At the same time through a variety of devices—full-scale press and radio campaigns, the manufacture of incidents, troop movements, carefully circulated rumours, and diplomatic leaks, a steadily mounting pressure was built up, timed to culminate in Hitler's long-awaited speech at the Nuremberg Party Congress. Those who study only the diplomatic documents get a very meagre impression of the war of nerves which was maintained throughout the summer and which was skilfully directed to play on the fear of war in Britain and France and to heighten the Czechs' sense of isolation. It was under the pressure of this political warfare, something very different from diplomacy as it had been traditionally practised, that the British and French governments felt themselves impelled to act.

What was Hitler's objective? The answer has been much confused by the ambiguous use of the word "war."

Western opinion made a clear-cut distinction between peace

and war: Hitler did not, he blurred the distinction. Reversing Clausewitz, he treated politics as a continuation of war by other means, at one stage of which (formally still called peace) he employed methods of political warfare subversion, propaganda, diplomatic and economic pressure, the war of nerves—at the next, the threat of war, and so on to localized war and up the scale to general war—a continuum of force in which the different stages ran into each other. Familiar enough now since the time of the Cold War, this strategy (which was all of a piece with Hitler's radical new style in foreign policy) was as confusing in its novelty as the tactics of the Trojan horse, the fifth column, and the "volunteers" to those who still thought in terms of a traditionally decisive break between a state of peace and a state of war.

So far as the events of 1938 go, there seem to be two possible answers to the question, What was in Hitler's mind?

The first is that his object was to destroy the Czech State by the sort of blitzkrieg for which he had rearmed Germany and which he was to carry out a year later against Poland. This was to come at the end of a six months' political, diplomatic, and propaganda campaign designed to isolate and undermine the Czechs, and to manoeuvre the Western Powers into abandoning them to their fate rather than risk a European war. The evidence for this view consists in the series of secret directives and the military preparations to which they led, plus Hitler's declaration on several occasions to the generals and his other collaborators that he meant to settle the matter by force, with 1 October as D-day. On this view, he was only prevented from carrying out his attack by the intervention of Chamberlain which, however great the cost to the Czechs, prevented war or at least postponed it for a year.

The other view is that Hitler never intended to go to war, that his objective was from the beginning a political settlement such as was offered to him at Munich, that his military preparations were not intended seriously but were designed as threats to increase the pressure.

The choice between these two alternatives, however—*either* the one *or* the other—seems to me unreal. The obvious course for Hitler to pursue was to keep both possibilities open to the very last possible moment, the more so since they did not conflict. The more seriously the military preparations were carried out, the more effective was the pressure in favour of a political settlement if at the last moment he decided not to take the risks involved in a military operation. If we adopt this view, then we remove all the difficulties in interpreting the evidence which are created either by attempting to pin Hitler down on any particular declaration and say *now*, at this point, he had decided on war—or by the dogmatic assumption that Hitler *never* seriously contemplated the use of force, with the consequent need to dismiss his military directives as bluff.

Neither in 1938 nor in 1939 did Hitler deliberately plan to start a general European war. But this was a risk which could not be ignored, and in 1938 it was decisive. The generals were unanimous that Germany's rearmament had not yet reached the point where she could face a war with France and Britain. The Czech frontier defences were formidable. Their army on mobilization was hardly inferior at all, either in numbers or training, to the thirty-seven divisions which the Germans could deploy and it was backed by a first-class armaments industry. To overcome these would require a concentration of force which left the German commander in the West with totally inadequate strength to hold back the French Army.

While the generals, however, added up divisions and struck an unfavourable balance in terms of material forces, Hitler was convinced that the decisive question was a matter of will, the balance between his determination to take the *risk* of a general war and the determination of the Western Powers, if pushed far enough, to take the *actual decision* of starting one. For, however much the responsibility for such a war might be Hitler's, by isolating the issue and limiting his demands to the Sudetenland, he placed the onus of actually starting a general war on the British and the French. How far was Hitler prepared to drive such an argument? The answer is, I believe, that while he had set a date by which he knew he must decide, until the very last moment he had not made up his mind and that it is this alternation between screwing up his demands, as he did at his second meeting with Chamberlain in Godesberg, and still evading an irrevocable decision, which accounts both for the zigzag course of German diplomacy and for the strain on Hitler.

In the end he decided, or was persuaded, to stop short of

military operations against Czechoslovakia and "cash" his military preparations for the maximum of political concessions.

No sooner had he agreed to this, however, than Hitler started to regret that he had not held on, marched his army in, then and there, and broken up the Czechoslovak State, not just annexed the Sudetenland. His regret sprang from the belief, confirmed by his meeting with the Western leaders at Munich, that he could have got away with a localized war carried out in a matter of days, and then confronted the British and French with a *fait accompli* while they were still hesitating whether to attack in the West—exactly as happened a year later over Poland.

Almost immediately after Munich, therefore, Hitler began to think about ways in which he could complete his original purpose. Every sort of excuse, however transparent, was found for delaying the international guarantee which had been an essential part of the Munich agreement. At the same time, the ground was carefully prepared with the Hungarians, who were eager to recover Ruthenia and at least part of Slovakia, and with the Slovaks themselves who were cast for the same role the Sudeten Germans had played the year before. The actual moment at which the crisis broke was not determined by Hitler and took him by surprise, but that was all. The Slovaks were at once prodded into declaring their independence and putting themselves in Hitler's hands. The Czech Government, after Hitler had threatened President Hacha in Berlin, did the same. The "legality" of German intervention was unimpeachable: Hitler had been invited to intervene by both the rebels and the government. War had been avoided, no shots exchanged, peace preserved—yet the independent state of Czechoslovakia had been wiped off the map.

IX

Within less than eighteen months, then, Hitler had successfully achieved both the immediate objectives, Austria and Czechoslovakia, which he had laid down in the Hossbach meeting. He had not foreseen the way in which this would happen, in fact he had been wrong about it, but this had not stopped him from getting both.

This had been true at every stage of Hitler's career. He had no fixed idea in 1930, even in 1932, about how he would become Chancellor, only that he would; no fixed idea in 1934–5 how he would break out of Germany's diplomatic isolation, again only that he would. So the same now. Fixity of aim by itself, or opportunism by itself, would have produced nothing like the same results.

It is entirely in keeping with this view of Hitler that, after Czechoslovakia, he should not have made up his mind what to do next. Various possibilities were in the air. Another move was likely in 1939, if only because the rearmament programme was now beginning to reach the period when it would give Germany a maximum advantage and Hitler had never believed that time was on his side. This advantage, he said in November 1937, would only last, at the most until 1943–5; then the other Powers with greater resources would begin to catch up. He had therefore to act quickly if he wanted to achieve his objectives.

Objectives, yes; a sense of urgency in carrying them out, and growing means to do so in German rearmament, but no time-table or precise plan of action for the next stage.

Ribbentrop had already raised with the Poles, immediately after Munich, the question of Danzig and the Corridor. But there is no evidence that Hitler had committed himself to war to obtain these, or to the dismemberment of Poland. If the Poles had been willing to give him what he wanted, Hitler might well have treated them, for a time at any rate, as a satellite—in much the same way as he treated Hungary—and there were strong hints from Ribbentrop that the Germans and the Poles could find a common objective in action against Russia. Another possibility, if Danzig and the Corridor could be settled by agreement, was to turn west and remove the principal obstacle to German expansion, the British and French claim to intervene in Eastern Europe.

After Prague, the German-Polish exchanges became a good deal sharper and, given the Poles' determination not to be put in the same position as the Czechs, but to say "No" and refuse to compromise, it is likely that a breach between Warsaw and Berlin would have come soon in any case. But what precipitated it was the British offer, and Polish acceptance, of a guarantee of

Poland's independence. In this sense the British offer is a turning-point in the history of 1939. But here comes the crux of the matter. If Mr. Taylor is right in believing that Hitler was simply an opportunist who reacted to the initiative of others, then he is justified in calling the British offer to Poland a revolutionary event. But if the view I have suggested is right, namely, that Hitler, although an opportunist in his tactics, was an opportunist who had from the beginning a clear objective in view, then it is very much less than that: an event which certainly helped—if you like, forced—Hitler to make up his mind between the various possibilities he had been revolving, but which certainly did not provoke him into an expansionist programme he would not otherwise have entertained, or generate the force behind it which the Nazis had been building up ever since they came to power. On this view it was Hitler who still held the initiative, as he had since the *Anschluss,* and the British who were reacting to it, not the other way round: the most the British guarantee did was to give Hitler the answer to the question he had been asking since Munich, Where next?

The answer, then, was Poland, the most probable in any event in view of the demands the Nazis had already tabled, and now a certainty. But this did not necessarily mean war—yet.

Hitler expressed his anger by denouncing Germany's Non-Aggression Pact with Poland and the Anglo-German Naval Treaty, and went on to sign a secret directive ordering the Army to be ready to attack Poland by 1 September. The military preparations were not bluff: they were designed to give Hitler the option of a military solution if he finally decided this way, or to strengthen the pressures for a political solution— either direct with Warsaw, or by the intervention of the other powers in a Polish Munich. Just as in 1938 so in 1939, Hitler kept the options open literally to the last, and until the troops actually crossed the Polish frontier on 1 September none of his generals was certain that the orders might not be changed. Both options, however: there is no more reason to say dogmatically that Hitler was aiming all the time at a political solution than there is to say that he ruled it out and had made up his mind in favour of war.

Hitler's inclination, I believe, was always towards a solution by force the sort of localized blitzkrieg with which in the end he did destroy Poland. What he had to weigh was the risk of a war which could not be localized. There were several reasons why he was more ready to take this risk than the year before.

The first was the progress of German rearmament—which was coming to a peak in the autumn of 1939. By then it represented an eighteen-fold expansion of the German armed forces since 1933. In economists' terms this was not the maximum of which Germany was capable, at least in the long run, but in military terms it was more than adequate, as 1940 showed, not just to defeat the Poles but to deal with the Western Powers as well. The new German Army had been designed to achieve the maximum effect at the outset of a campaign and Hitler calculated—quite rightly—that, even if the British formally maintained their guarantee to Poland, the war would be over and Poland crushed before they could do anything about it.

A second reason was Hitler's increased confidence, his conviction that his opponents were simply not his equal either in daring or in skill. The very fact that he had drawn back at Munich and then regretted it made it all the more likely that a man with his gambler's temperament would be powerfully drawn to stake all next time.

Finally, Hitler believed that he could remove the danger of Western intervention, or at least render the British guarantee meaningless, by outbidding the Western Powers in Moscow.

In moments of exaltation, e.g. in his talks to his generals after the signature of the Pact with Italy (23 May) and at the conference of 22 August which followed the news that Stalin would sign, Hitler spoke as if the matter were settled, war with Poland inevitable, and all possibility of a political settlement—on his terms—excluded. I believe that this was, as I have said, his real inclination, but I do not believe that he finally made up his mind until the last minute. Why should he? Just as in 1938, Hitler refused to make in advance the choice to which historians have tried to pin him down, the either/or of war or a settlement dictated under the threat of war. He fixed the date by which the choice would have to be made but pursued a course which would leave him with the maximum of manœuvre to the last possible moment. And again one may well ask, Why not—

since the preparations to be made for either eventuality—war or a political settlement under the threat of war—were the same?

Much has been made of the fact that for the greater part of the summer Hitler retired to Berchtesgaden and made no public pronouncement. But this is misleading. The initiative remained in Hitler's hands. The propaganda campaign went ahead exactly as planned, building up to a crisis by late August and hammering on the question, Is Danzig worth a war? So did the military preparations which were complete by the date fixed, 26 August. German diplomacy was mobilized to isolate Poland and, if the pact with Italy proved to be of very little value in the event, and the Japanese failed to come up to scratch, the pact with Stalin was a major coup. For a summer of "inactivity" it was not a bad result.

Hitler's reaction when the Nazi-Soviet Pact was signed shows clearly enough were his first choice lay. Convinced that the Western Powers would now give up any idea of intervention in defence of Poland, he ordered the German Army to attack at dawn on 26 August: i.e. a solution by force, but localized and without risk of a general European war, the sort of operation for which German rearmament had been designed from the beginning.

The unexpected British reaction, the confirmation instead of the abandonment of the guarantee to Poland—this, plus Mussolini's defection (and Mussolini at any rate had no doubt that Hitler was bent on a solution by force) upset Hitler's plans and forced him to think again. What was he to do? Keep up the pressure and hope that the Poles would crack and accept his terms? Keep up the pressure and hope that, if not the Poles, then the British would crack and either press the Poles to come to terms (another Munich) or abandon them? Or go ahead and take the risk of a general war, calculating that Western intervention, if it ever took place, would come too late to affect the outcome.

It is conceivable that if Hitler had been offered a Polish Munich, on terms that would by now have amounted to capitulation, he would still have accepted it. But I find it hard to believe that any of the moves he made, or sanctioned, between 25 August and 1 September were seriously directed to starting negotiations. A far more obvious and simple explanation is to say that, having failed to remove the threat of British intervention by the Nazi-Soviet Pact, as he had expected, Hitler postponed the order to march and allowed a few extra days to see, not if war could be avoided, but whether under the strain a split might not develop between the Western Powers and Poland and so leave the Poles isolated after all.

Now the crisis had come, Hitler himself did little to resolve or control it. Characteristically, he left it to others to make proposals, seeing the situation, not in terms of diplomacy and negotiation, but as a contest of wills. If his opponents' will cracked first, then the way was open for him to do what he wanted and march into Poland without fear that the Western Powers would intervene. To achieve this he was prepared to hold on and bluff up to the very last minute, but if the bluff did not come off within the time he had set, then this time he steeled his will to go through with the attack on Poland even if it meant running the risk of war with Britain and France as well. All the accounts agree on the strain which Hitler showed and which found expression in his haggard appearance and temperamental outbursts. But his will held. This was no stumbling into war. It was neither misunderstanding nor miscalculation which sent the German Army over the frontier into Poland, but a calculated risk, the gambler's bid—the only bid, Hitler once told Goering, he ever made, *va banque*, the bid he made when he reoccupied the Rhineland in 1936 and when he marched into Austria, the bid he had failed to make when he agreed to the Munich conference, only to regret it immediately afterwards.

X

Most accounts of the origins of the war stop in September 1939. Formally, this is correct: from 3 September 1939 Germany was in a state of war with Britain and France as well as Poland, and the Second World War had begun. But this formal statement is misleading. In fact, Hitler's gamble came off. The campaign in which the German Army defeated the Poles remained a localized war and no hostilities worth speaking of had taken place between Germany and the Western Powers by the time the Poles had been defeated and the state whose independence they had guaranteed had ceased to exist.

If Hitler had miscalculated at the beginning of September or stumbled into war without meaning to, here was the opportunity to avoid the worst consequences of what had happened. It is an interesting speculation what the Western Powers would have done, if he had really made an effort to secure peace once the Poles were defeated. But it is a pointless speculation. For Hitler did nothing of the sort. The so-called peace offer in his speech of 6 October was hardly meant to be taken seriously. Instead of limiting his demands, Hitler proceeded to destroy the Polish State and to set in train (in 1939, not in 1941) the ruthless resettlement programme which he had always declared he would carry out in Eastern Europe.

Even more to the point, it was Hitler who took the initiative in turning the formal state of war between Germany and the Western Powers into a real war. On 9 October he produced a memorandum in which he argued that, instead of waiting to see whether the Western Powers would back their formal declaration of war with effective force, Germany should seize the initiative and make an all-out attack on the French and the British, thereby removing once and for all the limitations on Germany's freedom of action.

The German generals saw clearly what this meant: far from being content with, and trying to exploit the good luck which had enabled him to avoid a clash with the Western Powers so far, Hitler was deliberately setting out to turn the localized campaign he had won in Poland into a general war. Their doubts did not deter him for a moment and, although they managed on one pretext or another to delay operations, in May 1940 it was the German Army, without waiting for the French or the British, which launched the attack in the West and turned the *drôle de guerre* into a major war.

Even this is not the end of the story. Once again, Hitler proved to be a better judge than the experts. In the middle of events, his nerve faltered, he became hysterical, blamed everyone, behaved in short in exactly the opposite way to the copybook picture of the man of destiny: but when the battle was over he had inflicted a greater and swifter defeat upon France than any in history. And it is no good saying that it was "the machine" that did this, not Hitler. Hitler was never the prisoner of "the machine." If "the machine" had been left to decide things, it would never have taken the risk of attacking in the West, and, if it had, would never have adopted the Ardennes plan which was the key to victory. Pushing the argument further back, one can add that, if it had been left to "the machine," German rearmament would never have been carried out at the pace on which Hitler insisted, or on the blitzkrieg pattern which proved to be as applicable to war with the Western Powers as to the limited Polish campaign.

Once again, the obvious question presents itself: what would have happened if Hitler, now as much master of continental Europe as Napoleon had been, had halted at this point, turned to organizing a continental New Order in Europe, and left to the British the decision whether to accept the situation—if not in 1940, then perhaps in 1941—or to continue a war in which they had as yet neither American nor Russian allies, were highly vulnerable to attack, and could never hope by themselves to overcome the disparity between their own and Hitler's continental resources. Once again—this is my point—it was thanks to Hitler, and no one else that this question was never posed. It was Hitler who decided that enough was not enough, that the war must go on—Hitler, not the German military leaders or the German people, many of whom would have been content to stop at this point, enjoy the fruits of victory, and risk nothing more.

If the war had to continue, then the obvious course was to concentrate all Germany's—and Europe's—resources on the one opponent left, Britain. If invasion was too difficult and dangerous an operation, there were other means—a Mediterranean campaign with something more than the limited forces reluctantly made available to Rommel, or intensification of the air and submarine war, as Raeder urged. The one thing no one thought of except Hitler was to attack Russia, a country whose government had shown itself painfully anxious to avoid conflict and give every economic assistance to Germany. There was nothing improvised about Hitler's attack on Russia. Of all his decisions it was the one taken furthest in advance and most carefully prepared for, the one over which he hesitated least and which he approached with so much confidence that he even risked a five-week delay in starting in order to punish the Yugoslavs and settle the Balkans.

Nor was it conceived of solely as a military operation. The plans were ready to extend to the newly captured territory the monstrous programme of uprooting whole populations which the S.S.—including Eichmann—had already put into effect in Poland. Finally, of all Hitler's decisions it is the one which most clearly bears his own personal stamp, the culmination (as he saw it) of his whole career.

XI

It will now be evident why I have carried my account beyond the conventional date of September 1939. Between that date and June 1941, the scope of the war was steadily enlarged from the original limited Polish campaign to a conflict which, with the attack on Russia, was now on as great a scale as the war of 1914–18. The initiative at each stage—except in the Balkans where he was reluctant to become involved—had been Hitler's. Of course he could not have done this without the military machine and skill in using it which the German armed forces put at his disposal, but the evidence leaves no doubt that the decision where and when to use that machine was in every case Hitler's, not his staff's, still less that all Hitler was doing was to react to the initiative of his opponents.

Now, it may be said that the Hitler who took these increasingly bold decisions after September 1939 was a different person from the Hitler who conducted German foreign policy before that date, but this is surely implausible. It seems to me far more likely that the pattern which is unmistakable after September 1939, using each victory as the basis for raising the stakes in a still bolder gamble next time, is the correct interpretation of his conduct of foreign policy before that date. And this interpretation is reinforced by the fact that at the same time Hitler was carrying out the rearmament and expansion of the German armed forces on a pattern which exactly corresponds to the kind of war which he proceeded to wage after September 1939.

Let me repeat and underline what I said earlier in this lecture: this has nothing to do with time-tables and blueprints of aggression. Throughout his career Hitler was an opportunist, prepared to seize on and exploit any opportunity that was offered to him. There was nothing inevitable about the way or the order in which events developed, either before or after September 1939. The annexation of Austria and the attempt to eliminate Czechoslovakia, by one means or another, were predictable, but after the occupation of Prague, there were other possibilities which might have produced a quite different sequence of events—as there were after the fall of France. Of what wars or other major events in history is this not true?

But Hitler's opportunism was doubly effective because it was allied with unusual consistency of purpose. This found expression in three things:

First, in his aims—to restore German military power, expand her frontiers, gather together the scattered populations of Volksdeutsche, and found a new German empire in Eastern Europe, the inhabitants of which would either be driven out, exterminated, or retained as slave-labour.

Second, in the firmness with which he grasped from the beginning what such aims entailed—the conquest of power in Germany on terms that would leave him with a free hand, the risk of pre-emptive intervention by other Powers, the need to shape German rearmament in such a way as to enable him to win a quick advantage within a limited time by surprise and concentration of force, the certainty that to carry out his programme would mean war.

Third, in the strength of will which underlay all his hesitations, opportunism, and temperamental outbursts, and in his readiness to take risks and constantly to increase these by raising the stakes—from the reoccupation of the Rhineland to the invasion of Russia (with Britain still undefeated in his rear) within the space of no more than five years.

Given such an attitude on the part of a man who controlled one of the most powerful nations in the world, the majority of whose people were prepared to believe what he told them about their racial superiority and to greet his satisfaction of their nationalist ambitions with enthusiasm—given this, I cannot see how a clash between Germany and the other Powers could have been avoided. Except on the assumption that Britain and France were prepared to disinterest themselves in what happened east of the Rhine and accept the risk of seeing him create a German hegemony over the rest of Europe. There was nothing inevitable about either the date or the issue on which the clash actually came. It half came over Czechoslovakia in 1938; it might have come over another issue than Poland. But I cannot see how it could have been avoided some time, somewhere, un-less the other Powers were prepared to stand by and watch Hitler pursue his tactics of one-at-a-time to the point where they would no longer have the power to stop him.

If the Western Powers had recognized the threat earlier and shown greater resolution in resisting Hitler's (and Mussolini's) demands, it is possible that the clash might not have led to war, or at any rate not to a war on the scale on which it had finally to be fought. The longer they hesitated, the higher the price of resistance. This is their share of the responsibility for the war: that they were reluctant to recognize what was happening, reluctant to give a lead in opposing it, reluctant to act in time. Hitler understood their state of mind perfectly and played on it with skill. None of the Great Powers comes well out of the history of the 1930s, but this sort of responsibility even when it runs to appeasement, as in the case of Britain and France, or complicity in the case of Russia, is still recognizably different from that of a government which deliberately creates the threat of war and sets out to exploit it.

In the Europe of the 1930s there were several leaders—Mus-solini, for instance—who would have liked to follow such a policy, but lacked the toughness of will and the means to carry it through. Hitler alone possessed the will and had provided himself with the means. Not only did he create the threat of war and exploit it, but when it came to the point he was prepared to take the risk and go to war and, then when he had won the Polish campaign, to redouble the stakes and attack again, first in the West, then in the East. For this reason, despite all that we have learned since of the irresolution, shabbiness, and chicanery of other governments' policies, Hitler and the nation which followed him still bear, not the sole, but the primary responsibil-ity for the war which began in 1939 and which, before Hitler was prepared to admit defeat, cost the lives of more than 25 million human beings in Europe alone.

Conclusion

It is now over ten years since the publication of the *Origins*. Although tempers have cooled, it is probably safe to say that Mr. Taylor's critics would probably still write in the same vein, or at least would not seriously modify their positions. This is not because of obstinance, but conviction. Obviously the critics have strong disagreements among themselves, but one should not expect a general consensus on such a controversial issue. As Professor Alfred Gollin has written, "historical conclusions need not be in agreement; different historians can do their work well and yet disagree; different generations and, indeed, different people prefer or accept different conclusions and that is why history and the study of it is so fascinating—why it lives."

On one point in particular there does appear to be a consensus of the critics—that where Mr. Taylor is wrongheaded is not so much in his specific judgment about Hitler as in his belief—or so interpreted by the critics—that wars are never intended but are due to the blunderings of diplomats. As Geoffrey Hudson has pointed out, the idea that men are never knaves, but only fools, is perhaps good liberalism, since it affirms the goodness, if not the intelligence, of human beings, but this idea does not correspond to the realities of human history. It is simply a fact that some political leaders do pursue aims that can be achieved by violence and they are ready to use violence to achieve those aims. Hitler pursued goals that could be won only by violence and the German people followed him. Since Mr. Taylor agrees with that line of reasoning (his ideas are explicit in "Second Thoughts")

147

it is perhaps unfortunate that he framed the argument of the book in such a way as to be profoundly misunderstood on the issues of causes of war and responsibility for war. In his own words, however, "My only mistake was not to emphasize more clearly that I was writing about the origins of the minor European conflict which broke out in 1939, not about the origins of the real Second World War." On the specific subject of the *Origins* that remains most controversial—Hitler's war aims in 1939—Mr. Taylor may have the final say. In his masterpiece, *English History, 1914–1945*, published four years after the *Origins,* he wrote: "Hitler, it seems to me, had no precise plans of aggression, only an intention, which he held in common with most Germans, to make Germany again the most powerful state in Europe and a readiness to take advantage of events. I am confident that the truth of this interpretation will be recognized once the problem is discussed in terms of detached historical curiosity, and not of political commitment."

Suggestions for Further Reading

Important critiques of the *Origins* not reproduced in this symposium are cited by Robert Spencer, "War Unpremeditated?" *Canadian Historical Review*, June 1962. This article synthesizes the major ideas generated by the controversy and makes a valuable evaluation of the book itself. T. W. Manson, "Some Origins of the Second World War," *Past and Present*, December 1964, considers the controversy in relation to Germany's prewar economy and comments on Mr. Taylor's use of Burton H. Klein's *Germany's Economic Preparations for War* (Harvard University Press, 1959). See also P. A. Reynolds, "Hitler's War," *History* (1961–1962), which takes Mr. Taylor to task for errors of detail as well as interpretation. There is also an important review in the *Annals of the American Academy* (May 1962) by the revisionist Harry Elmer Barnes, who was virtually the only American critic to review the book with complete enthusiasm.* Or Mr. Taylor's philosophy of history and the *Origins,* see the "profile" in the *Observer,* April 16, 1961, and Ved Mehta, *Fly and the Fly-Bottle: Encounters with British Intellectuals* (Boston ?1963).

The impact of the *Origins* in German intellectual circles can be followed in the following critiques.

Josef Engel, "Zeitgeschichte—Aussenpolitik," *Geschichte in Wissenschaft und Unterricht,* 14 (1963), pp. 517–32.

---

* This and other important critiques do not appear in the symposium because of failure to obtain permission from owners of copyright.

Ulrich Mohl, "Die Kriegsschuldfrage in neuer Sicht: Gewagte Thesen des britischen Historikers A. J. P. Taylor," *Geschichte in Wissenschaft und Unterricht*, 13 (1962), pp. 713–717.

Golo Mann, "Hitlers britischer Advokat," *Der Monat*, 13 (1961), pp. 79–86.

Gotthard Jasper, "Über die Ursachen des Zweiten Weltkrieges; Zu den Büchern von A. J. P. Taylor und David L. Hoggan," *Vierteljahreshefte für Zeitgeschichte*, 10 (1962), pp. 311–340.

Wolfgang Bingeser, "Taylors Hitlerbild," *Aussenpolitik*, 14 (1963), p. 72.

Heinrich Bodensieck, "Antithesen zur Vorgeschichte des Zweiten Weltkrieges?", *Neue Politische Literatur*, 7 (1962), pp. 381–98.

"Adolf Hitler—Weder Held noch Schurke?," *Der Spiegel*, November 22, 1961.

Hans-Günther Seraphim, "Zur Vorgeschichte des Zweiten Weltkrieges," *Das historisch-politische Buch*, 10 (1962), pp. 161–64.

See also the articles cited by Elizabeth Wiskemann, above, pp. 36–37. Two important commentaries in a leading French periodical are: F. Ryszka, "Les Origines de la Deuxième Guerre Mondiale," *Histoire de la Deuxième Guerre Mondiale* (October 1965); and P. M. H. Bell, "Hitler et les Origines de la Seconde Guerre Mondiale," ibid., July 1967.

Specific issues of the *Origins* controversy are discussed by Christopher Thorne, *The Approach of War 1938–39* (London, 1967), and D. C. Watt, "Appeasement: The Rise of a Revisionist School?", *Political Quarterly* (April, 1965). See also Martin Gilbert and Richard Gott, *The Appeasers* (London, 1963), a book dedicated to Mr. Taylor. Also, Keith Robbins, *Munich 1938* (London, 1968).

Since this book was compiled, three other pertinent works have appeared: Esmonde M. Robertson, ed., *The Origins of the Second World War* (London, 1971); Keith Eubank, *The Origins of World War II* (New York, 1969); and an important essay about Mr. Taylor by H. Russell Williams in *Historians of Modern Europe,* Hans A. Schmitt, ed. (Louisiana State Press, 1971). All of these works have their merits, but none attempt the precise purpose of this one—to focus directly on the controversy aroused by Mr. Taylor's *Origins of the Second World War*.